CHRISTIAN EDUCATION
IN THE
AFRICAN AMERICAN CHURCH

A GUIDE FOR TEACHING TRUTH

CHRISTIAN EDUCATION

IN THE

AFRICAN AMERICAN CHURCH

A GUIDE FOR TEACHING TRUTH

LORA-ELLEN McKINNEY

FOREWORD BY JOHNNY RAY YOUNGBLOOD

JUDSON PRESS · VALLEY FORGE

Christian Education in the African American Church:
A Guide for Teaching Truth

Library of Congress Cataloging-in-Publication Data

McKinney, Lora-Ellen.
    Christian education in the African American church : a guide for teaching truth / Lora-Ellen McKinney.
        p. cm.
        Includes bibliographical references.
        ISBN 0-8170-1450-0 (pbk. : alk. paper)
1. African American churches. 2. Christian education. I. Title.

BR563.N4 M352 2003
268'.089'9607—dc21

2002040731

Printed in the U.S.A.

09 08 07 06 05 04 03

10 9 8 7 6 5 4 3 2 1

To my mother, Louise,
who loves, teaches, and encourages me

CONTENTS

LORA-ELLEN McKINNEY HAS WRITTEN THE CHRISTIAN EDUCATION classic of the future for the African American church or any other church that serves African Americans. This salient work is profound and not pious. It is substantive and still spiritual.

Dr. McKinney writes this book with an undeniable sense of authority. "By what authority" does she pen these pages? First, she is a child of the manse, a "PK" (pastor's kid). Second, she has paid her dues in the halls of academia and is an active member in a productive ministry. Third, she is committed to excellent Christian education because she was a Sunday school dropout at the age of nine, the result of teachers whose minds were closed to inquiry.

I would tout Dr. McKinney as a critical lover of the African American church, who by way of this work evidences her love for Christ and church and culture.

Section One of *Christian Education in the African American Church: A Guide for Teaching Truth* declares the indispensability of Christian education in the life and work of the church; that is, regardless of one's definition, church worship and Christian education are inseparable for the equipping of the saints. What Dr. McKinney says clearly is that Christian education ought to be no longer postscripted to the mission of the church.

What a challenge Section Two is to those who desire to stand forth as teachers of the life and ministry of the Lord of the church, and by this I do not exclude the pastor. Were a pastor to take Section Two as a preparation course for preaching and administering to a congregation, it would enhance sermon preparation as well as our administrative planning. Brother and sister pastors, brother and sister Christian educators, let's take the McKinney challenge!

Sections Three and Four are a sheer delight, for we are provided with existing examples of Christian education in process, as well as creative possibilities offered by Dr. McKinney herself, based on love, experience, and genius. If you seriously want to strengthen the ministry given you by the Holy Spirit, read this book for yourself and then put it in the hands of others to be read and realized.

Dr. Lora-Ellen McKinney has wrought a great work. We, both clergy and Christian educators, do ourselves and our constituency harm if we fail to pick up this gauntlet.

Rev. Dr. Johnny Ray Youngblood
Senior Pastor
Saint Paul's Community Baptist Church
Brooklyn, New York

INTRODUCTION

JESUS WAS A TEACHER. AMONG HIS OTHER ESSENTIAL ROLES IN THE course of doing his Father's business, Christ focused on providing his followers with a blueprint for living. That blueprint, found in the New Testament, provides Christian believers with guidelines for living and with a vital challenge to apply Jesus' teachings as the only method for building a solid foundation for earthly and eternal life.

While that solid foundation is most certainly built on faith, it also requires information, information that Jesus provided through explanations of law and **theology,** memorable stories (**parables**), models for prayer (Matthew 6:9-14) and for living, and evidence of his **divinity.** In the Sermon on the Mount (The Beatitudes, found in Matthew 5:1-10), in more than forty recorded parables, in interactions with the people of God, through his personal challenges, and in his death and resurrection, Jesus teaches us.

The teachings of Christ were and continue to be controversial. Jesus understood that, because of this, following him is not an automatic act. Instead, for each of us it is a deliberate, conscious, and important choice (Matthew 6:21), a choice requiring an understanding of the commitment that we make when we give our lives to Christ (Matthew 10:22). This, then, informs our role as Christian educators. We are charged with the awesome responsibility of explaining the blueprint that Christ has provided for us to those new to the faith and to those continuing, as we are, on the path of a life built with Christ as its foundation and center. Above all else, Christian education is ministry. According to Israel Galindo, author of *The Craft of Christian Teaching,* "done well, [Christian education] has the potential beyond any other congregational influence to deepen faith and commitment."[1]

As Christians, we have a charge to keep: to go into all the world and bring souls to Christ. Meeting this goal takes preparation. Our churches require trained and committed clergy in the pulpit and laity in the pews who, together as a Christian community, are willing and able to win the world for Christ. Excellent Christian education enhances our ability to obey the Great Commission. It is our best method for utilizing the finest tools of education and technology to increase the capacity of God's people to live and work effectively for him. "Jesus called his followers 'the salt of the earth' (a source of taste and preservation) and 'the light of the world' (an object of everyone's attention). Clearly, Jesus was expecting to see some changes in the lives of those who believed in him."[2] Jesus wanted us to know him so that we could live effectively for him.

As African American Christians we have an additional set of responsibilities. "As servants in a servant church, we are called to a ministry of liberation and reconciliation in the church of Jesus Christ."[3] In Christian education African American Christians view opportunities for healing and health, the reclamation of community, and the reinstallation of African-centered values into individual, family, and collective functioning.

Christian Education in the African American Church: A Guide for Teaching Truth discusses the craft, commitment, and context of Christian teaching by and for African Americans. Designed to assist pastors, worship leaders, directors of Christian education departments, and directors and teachers of Sunday school, church seminars and other classes, this book will present:

- The history of Christian education as a discipleship tool in African American churches
- Traditional and nontraditional forms of Christian education (Sunday school, seminars and workshops, counseling ministries, worship and sermonic teaching)
- The best practices in Christian education (including case studies and examples from a variety of churches throughout the United States)
- Ideas about how to succeed in a number of formats for Christian education
- Ideas about African-centered approaches to Christian education
- Recommendations for effective teaching to learners at different developmental stages

Christian Education in the African American Church: A Guide for Teaching Truth is divided into four sections. They are:

Section One: The Importance of Christian Education. This section defines Christian education and discusses its vital role in successful ministry, focusing on its traditional and innovative uses within the context of the African American church.

Section Two: Basic Teaching Skills and Learning Strategies. This section summarizes contemporary principles of effective teaching and typical modes of learning, applying this knowledge for use in programs designed for different age groups and ability classifications.

Section Three: Succeeding in a Variety of Christian Education Venues and Formats. This section provides guidance and tips related to delivering Christian education in the variety of formats, worship, and training opportunities available to any church.

Section Four: Building a Successful African-Centered Christian Education Program. This section focuses on recommendations for setting an effective program in motion and ways to evaluate the success of Christian education in the local church.

Each section of *Christian Education in the African American Church: A Guide for Teaching Truth* includes:

Teachable Moments: boxed recommendations from churches doing innovative work in Christian education that can serve as models for readers

Top Ten Lists: recommendations that can serve as easy references for understanding the centrality of Christian education to doing effective ministry, teaching Christians of all ages, identifying and enhancing Christian education offerings, and making certain that Christian education programs meet church missions

Preparation for the Journey: questions to guide Christian educators in refining their programs

References: books and websites to assist Christian educators with developing and enhancing their programs, with teaching a variety of students, and with thinking creatively about the definition and implementation of Christian education programs in the local church

Appendices provide additional information that may be useful to Christian educators:

Appendix 1: Africans in the Bible. A chart listing persons of African origins who appear in Scripture, including the relevant biblical reference and teaching theme that emerges from that person or group's story

Appendix 2: Prayer for All Africans. A prayer poem written for persons of African descent, whether Christian or of some other faith

Appendix 3: Christian Education Conferences. A list of conferences within African American denominations and related contact information

Appendix 4: Survey Letter. A copy of the letter that was sent to churches asking them to define Christian education and to provide examples of their most innovative Christian education programs

Appendix 5: Church Survey Respondents. A list of the churches that responded to the informal survey and some basic information about each congregation, including denominational affiliation, membership, and region

Appendix 6: Christian Education Survey Participants. More detailed information about the survey respondents, including contact information and the individual Christian educators who participated in the survey

Glossary: A word list to encourage new teachers of Christian education; terms included in the glossary will appear in bold typeface in the text

Finally, the purpose of this book is simple: to strengthen our opportunities to provide excellent Christian education within congregations of any African American denomination (as well as for African Americans worshipping in other Christian contexts). I am committed to assisting in the development of congregations that are well informed and African-centered in a manner that enhances their ability to live their lives and do God's work according to Christian principles. Christian education, I believe, informs us of Christ's purpose for our lives, teaches Christ's truths, provides us with tools for living in a purposeful and Christ-centered manner, surrounds us with Christ's love, and ultimately has the potential for saving our souls. Salvation, I believe, is more than the moment that we give our lives to Christ. It is, in fact, a process: We are saved and are being saved by God's grace in each moment of our lives. Christian education, at its best, is an aid to this process.

I am hopeful that *Christian Education in the African American Church: A Guide for Teaching Truth* will serve as a useful tool for developing, supporting, augmenting, and enhancing Christian education programs and strategies in African American churches.

To God be the glory!

Notes

1. *Israel Galindo.* The Craft of Christian Teaching: Essentials for Becoming a Very Good Teacher. *Valley Forge: Judson Press, 1998, page 4.*

2. *Stan Campbell and James S. Bell Jr.* The Complete Idiot's Guide to the Bible. *Alpha Books: A Pearson Education Company, 1999, page 200.*

3. *J. Deotis Roberts.* Africentric Christianity: A Theological Appraisal for Ministry. *Valley Forge: Judson Press, 2000, page 77.*

THE IMPORTANCE OF
CHRISTIAN EDUCATION

MAKING CHRIST LIVE IN US

The Relevance of Christian Education in Today's Church

The educational task of the [black church] is to teach its membership the theological underpinnings of a faith heritage that made real the hope of the Christian gospel for black people. Essentially, this is the mission of Christian education and the focus of evangelism in the black church.[1]

CHRISTIAN EDUCATION IS, ABOVE ALL ELSE, A PROCESS THAT HELPS a community of believers understand theology, learn Christian history, reinforce personal decisions to live for Christ, and make commitments to the internal and outreach ministries of the local church. People join the church for a variety of reasons, among which are the ability to be part of a community of like believers, to worship God, to learn the teachings of Christ, and to gain guidance for their lives. "We long for a system of beliefs and values that will help us cope with injustice, affirm human dignity, hope for a brighter future, and navigate a safe and satisfying course through life."[2] Christ provides this for us.

To fully understand and access the love of Christ, we must know him. To know him we must study him and learn, through direct instruction, private study, and corporate worship, the meaning and import of his word, in its historical form and as its applies to our daily lives. It is also essential that we, as African Americans, learn that Christianity is not a slave faith, some shameful remnant of our unlawful servitude on America's shores. In their book *Defending Black Faith: Answers to Tough Questions About African-American Christianity,* Craig S. Keener and Glenn Usry provide an array of well-researched facts that demonstrate that North Africa was "thoroughly Christianized" by the end of the second century. Additionally, from the beginning of the Christian mission, Christianity grew in the southern African land known as Nubia. The first Gentile Christian was, in fact, an Ethiopian official in the court of Queen Candace (Acts 8:27).[3] This research allows us to understand that, when Africans were eventually brought to the United States centuries later, some were likely to have been previously exposed to Christianity.

For enslaved Africans unfamiliar with Christianity, there was nonetheless a meaningful connection to their religious traditions. "When African slaves were introduced to the Bible, they were able to derive meaning from it that was hidden to their oppressors. They understood God against the background of traditional beliefs in a Supreme God. They were aware of the power and moral integrity of God. Jehovah, as described in the Old Testament, was a close facsimile of the African supreme being they had known."[4]

"Christian education, then, takes on a new importance. Done well, it has the potential beyond any other congregational influence to deepen faith and commitment. Knowledge of its importance makes the need for educational revitalization all the more urgent. There is much work to be done."[5] In the African American context, Christian education has the capacity to teach us about Christ through a meaningful connection with our heritage, to debunk myths about our faith, and to teach values that apply to our lives as Africans in America. To do this well in a society that highly values entertainment and in which, it is reported, attention spans have decreased significantly, African American Christian educators must design theologically based, informative, and challenging programs that address the varied learning needs of parishioners and are meaningful, relevant, enjoyable, engaging, interesting, African-centered in their approach, and, most importantly, focused on Christ.

Christian Education Defined

So what is Christian education, and what role does it play in building a successful ministry? The goal of education of any kind is to nurture in students an understanding of concepts, themes, philosophies, and facts, hopefully with an expectation that this knowledge will be applicable to their lives. Christian education has a similar goal with one notable exception: It is an educational process that produces Christians. Christian education seeks to develop in its learners a strong belief in, dedication to, and knowledge of Jesus Christ so they can better know him, reflect his image in the world, and bring others to him.

In the African American context, Christian education also provides hope and opportunity. The African American pulpit speaks "with great force and fortitude to the sinful social structures and the perpetuators of an unjust social and economic system. It impel[s] the victims [of oppression and injustice] to rise up and to participate in God's plan for their redemption."[6] The modern African American church understands that, despite the many advances made in achieving social equity, injustice remains real to its members. As a result, African Americans empathize with the suffering of Jesus and his triumphs over enemies and the grave. Identifying with the manner in which he has provided protection, salvation, and amazing grace, we work to overcome our spiritual barriers so that the redemption offered by Jesus is available to us in this world and the next.

Though the Word of God is stable and eternal, local congregations have unique and individualized ways of defining Christian education and providing programs that meet the specific learning needs of their congregations. For example, recognizing that the majority of their congregation is comprised of new Christians, many of whom are young adults who represent the second or third generation of unchurched persons in their families, the University Park Baptist Church of Charlotte, North Carolina, designs Christian education curricula and courses that address the learning needs and attract the interest of Generation-X Christians.

To determine a functional definition of Christian education used in the programs of black churches, this book's author sent letters to a number of churches around the country (see Appendix 4) in an attempt to balance African American denominations (AME, AME Zion, Baptist, Church of God in Christ), geographical regions (East, Northeast, Midwest, South, West, Pacific Northwest), and church size

4

(congregations from 250 to 28,000). Pastors and directors of Christian education were asked their definitions of Christian education. Some of their responses follow.[7]

[The purpose of Christian education is] to provide biblically based programs, resources, and support within the church and community that will meet needs, transform lives, and prepare individuals for every good Christian service.

—Rev. Nadine Burton, Associate Pastor Christian Education,
Mississippi Boulevard Christian Church, Memphis, Tennessee

Christian education is the means of educating Christians. While this may appear to be circular in thought, it is not. Too often we limit Christian education to biblical and theological realms. Many, for example, think of it only in terms of Sunday school. It must extend far beyond this. We live in a multifaceted society that is becoming more global every day. [We must] educate Christians not to ignore or become like the prevailing society. Instead we seek to empower them to be ready and able to effectively engage the society and its cultures.... The world is seeking answers and we in the body of Christ must mature to be just that—the answers. It is through holistic Christian education that this occurs.

—Elder Vincent Harrison, Senior Director of Education,
New Birth Missionary Baptist Church, Lithonia, Georgia

Christian education is a lifelong discipleship process that is experienced in family life, worship, Bible study and other course study, counseling, training and equipping opportunities, conferences, seminars, mission experiences, and recreational experiences. Discipleship is not a one-time event. It is a dynamic, ever-evolving, ever-changing process with the central focus being God's Word. The needs of the audience may change but teaching should always lead to intentional, diligent application within the lives of contemporary Christians.

—Dr. Cassandra Aline Jones, Minister of Assimilation (New Members),
University Park Baptist Church, Charlotte, North Carolina

Christian education is "connected education," or "conversational education," writes Carol Lakey Hess in Education As an Art of Getting Dirty with Dignity. In her writing she identifies "three curricula" that all church institutions teach: (a) the explicit, (b) the implicit, and (c) the null curriculum. African American church education must be conversational, including "discourse and exploration, talking and listening, questions, argument, speculation and sharing."

The theological basis of African American church education must be of a God who is relational and incarnational, ready to get down and dirty in the enterprise of reconciliation. This God is primarily revealed in the creation, covenant, and consummation narratives of the Bible.

Through hard dialogue and deep connections, would-be disciples must be taught to quest for true humanity in the image of God. The Church must teach African American girls and boys to assert themselves, especially for peace with justice. She must promote attitudes and processes that demonstrate courage to struggle and engage in conflict for the sake of genuine freedom within the beloved community. In her education she must include stories that expose violence, exploitation, and racism against people of color, while asserting human rights.

—Rev. Dr. James McCray Jr., Senior Pastor,
Jones United Methodist Church, San Francisco, California

Christian education is about discipleship, using our ministries to train people to become active representatives of the kingdom of God.
—Rev. George Mensah, Director of Christian Education,
Shiloh Baptist Church, Washington, D.C.

Christian education is the process by which people are prepared to become effective disciples of and witnesses for Jesus Christ.
—Rev. Dr. Samuel Berry McKinney, Pastor Emeritus,
Mount Zion Baptist Church, Seattle, Washington

Christian education is responsible for the religious development of the entire congregation, in accordance with the policies and procedures of

the AME Church department of Christian education and the editorial division, with the concurrence of the pastor.
—Rev. Joyce Randall, Minister of Christian Education,
First AME Church, Los Angeles, California

Christian education, in its simplest form is the educational teaching development designed to transform the life of the Christ-like student or learner. However, as we move forward in this millennium, just as we look at new definitions and new paradigms of learning, development, preaching, and teaching in the faith community, we must also look for the new "push" and transition in terminology in Christian education. Thus, we have, along with numerous other persons in the faith community, transitioned our language from that of "Christian education" to that of discipleship. They both have the [same] goal, but because of our consumer, microwave society, we must stay on the cutting edge of clarity of call, vision, and definition.
—Rev. Barbara Peacock, Minister of Discipleship,
University Park Baptist Church, Charlotte, North Carolina

Christian education is teaching people to lead a God-centered life through Bible study and how to best apply biblical principles to all aspects of their lives.
—Rev. Dr. James Perkins, Senior Pastor,
Greater Christ Baptist Church, Detroit, Michigan

Christian education is the entire educational program of the church.
—Rev. Dr. Jeremiah A. Wright Jr., Senior Pastor,
Trinity United Church of Christ, Chicago, Illinois

Though consistent in their aims, this range of definitions makes it clear that the effective education of African American Christians requires building the church of God through the development of a strong and knowledgeable Christian community. Churches are strengthened by members who understand the basic **tenets** of their faith, are clear about the commitment they have made to live for Christ (Matthew 18:18-20), are dedicated to working together to fulfill the Church's mission within their local congregation and in the world, are proud of their history as Christians of African origin, and are focused on serving the needs of the African American people within and outside the church.

One of the teachers of the law came and heard them debating. Noticing that Jesus had given them a good answer, he asked him, "Of all the commandments, which is the most important?"

"The most important one," answered Jesus, "is this: 'Hear, O Israel, the Lord our God, the Lord is one. Love the Lord your God with all your heart and with all your soul and with all your mind and with all your strength.' The second is this: 'Love your neighbor as yourself.' There is no commandment greater than these." (Mark 12:28-31)

How, then, do we educate Christians about the love of Christ and the admonitions of Mark 12:30 to love God completely? How do we address the particular history and needs of African American Christians? How do we understand Christian education within an African American context?

The Relevance of Christian Education to the African American Church

"Although most were not yet Christians when our ancestors came from Africa, some believed in only one God; most believed in many gods and spirits but acknowledged one supreme God who ruled over all. In the subsequent, distinctive experience of African Americans, we have found a special strength in the black church that has enabled us to stand against oppression."[8]

As the central and most enduring institution in the black community, the African American church has shepherded its flock from slavery to civil rights gained in a number of social and economic arenas. Historically, "not only did [the African American church] give birth to new institutions such as schools, banks, insurance companies, and low income housing, it also provided an academy and an arena for political activities, and it nurtured young talent for musical, dramatic, and artistic endeavors."[9] While continuing these efforts, today's African American church works to identify and provide for the needs of its congregation and the local community.

Rev. Rocky Miskelly, a consultant on church growth, notes that the role of the church in society has changed significantly over the last thirty years. The church used to be central to community life, and its members were unquestioningly loyal to it. Today's church exists in a society in which religion is less valued. The church has moved to the periphery of society and many members, less loyal to the institution, now look to the church to meet their specific needs (e.g., for healing, for entertainment, for proximity, for life partners).[10]

While African American churches remain more central to their communities than is the case with churches in other American racial and ethnic sectors, they too must be increasingly aware of who is sitting in their pews, what history of Christian observance they bring with them (African-centered, aware of and responsive to African American history, or followers of Eurocentric religious traditions that occur within an African American religious context), and their knowledge about, commitment to, and expectations of the church. Most importantly, the relevance of African American Christian education requires that church leaders believe that education is vital to the life of the church, have a commitment to build a program that reflects excellence in its execution, and are dedicated to the development of a body of Christ that is well-equipped to understand and embrace the rich fullness of its Afri-Christian history.

The Christian education focus of the African American church is tied to all of its ministries and activities as well as to its assessment of its congregation's educational needs. As is noted in the quote that opens the chapter and in the definitions provided by the author's informal survey, in the black context, Christian education teaches theology and helps Christians develop the skills to be strong disciples of and effective witnesses for Christ. To keep Christian education relevant to the African American church, Christian educators must know their Afri-Christian history so that their congregations can be grounded in the true history of their faith. Black churches must also maintain their broad educational objectives while adapting curricula, making content decisions, and basing teaching strategies on the needs of each unique congregation.

TEACHABLE MOMENT

Statistics on African American Worship[11]

○ African Americans are more likely than whites to report that they have prayed to God during the past 7 days. 93% of African Americans reported praying compared to 80% of white adults nationwide (2001).

○ African Americans are significantly more likely than are whites to have read from their Bible in the past 7 days (52% to 35%, respectively) (2001).

○ 43% of African Americans attend church on a given Sunday, which is similar to the rate of church attendance among whites (42%) (2001).

○ African Americans are approximately twice as likely as are whites to report that they are "searching for meaning and purpose in life" (58% to 28%, respectively) (2001).

○ African Americans are more likely than average to say that they are "born again Christians," a belief held by 57% of African Americans compared to 39% of adults nationwide (2001).

○ 21% of the African American population is unchurched, compared to 32% of whites (1998).

○ Compared to 66% of whites, 83% of blacks say their religious faith is very important in their lives (2001).

○ 46% of African Americans feel that they have a responsibility to tell other people about their religious beliefs; 33% of whites feel the same way (2001).

Making Disciples

Disciples are followers of Christ. Disciples of Christ believe in his Word and strive to live according to his dictates. "Since the 'making of disciples' constitutes the ultimate goal of [our churches], we must facilitate that end through consistent and creative, intentional and insightful, rigorous and enriching, practical and promising, cultural and contextual means of teaching 'all persons' the fulfilling life, uniquely discovered through Christian education."[12]

Christ envisions the church as a community of like believers who support each other in our walks of faith. However, being supportive requires that we clearly understand what Christ expects of us. "Disciplemaking ensures that the gospel is embedded deeply in the lives of mature believers who serve as links to the future. Discipling then is a relationship where we intentionally walk alongside a growing disciple or disciples in order to encourage, correct, and challenge them in love to grow toward maturity in Christ."[13] Christian education is a means to this end.

As Christians it is our duty to "grow in the grace and knowledge of our Lord and Savior Jesus Christ" (2 Peter 3:18). Doing so requires that we have an understanding of the unique learning needs of an individual church and the commitment of that church to providing excellent Christian education classes and resources for its members. As one Christian educator aptly states, "a stable church is a growing church. A stable Christian is a growing Christian. A growing Christian is an educated Christian."[14] An educated African-centered Christian is one who grows in his or her understanding of Christ within the context of a history that includes Africans—in the Bible, in the early spread of Christianity, in their early experiences in America, and in the challenges and triumphs of our modern survival. This information solidifies Christ's promise that in him we are all victors (1 Corinthians 15:57, 1 John 5:4).

Notes

1. *Dr. Forrest Harris.* Theology from a Black Baptist Perspective. *Seminar VI, Ministers' Division of the National Baptist Congress of Christian Education, St. Louis, Missouri, June 17–21, 2002, page 129.*

2. *Stan Campbell and James S. Bell Jr.* The Complete Idiot's Guide to the Bible. *Alpha Books: A Pearson Education Company, 1999, "Foreword."*

3. *Craig S. Keener and Glenn Usry.* Defending Black Faith: Answers to Tough Questions About African-American Christianity. *Downers Grove, Illinois: Intervarsity Press, 1997, page 14.*

4. *Latta R. Thomas, quoted by J. Deotis Roberts.* Africentric Christianity: A Theological Appraisal for Ministry. *Valley Forge: Judson Press, 2000, page 47.*

5. *Israel Galindo.* The Craft of Christian Teaching: Essentials for Becoming a Very Good Teacher. *Valley Forge: Judson Press, 1998, page 18.*

6. *Olin P. Moyd.* The Sacred Art: Preaching and Theology in the African American Tradition. *Valley Forge: Judson Press, 1995, page 5.*

7. *These quotations are from phone and e-mail interviews conducted between April and August 2002.*

8. *Craig S. Keener and Glenn Usry.* Black Man's Religion: Can Christianity Be Afrocentric? *Downers Grove, Illinois: Intervarsity Press, 1996, page 18.*

9. *C. Eric Lincoln and Lawrence H. Mamiya.* The Black Church in the African American Experience. *Durham, N.C.: Duke University Press, 1990, page 8.*

10. *Rocky Miskelly. Cargill Associates, lecture at leadership retreat, Chantilly, Virginia, 2002.*

11. *Barna Research, www.barna.org (accessed September 10, 2002). Archives: African Americans.*

12. *Alvin Christopher Bernstine.* How to Develop a Department of Christian Education within the Local Baptist Church: A Congregational Enablement Model. *Nashville: Townsend Press, 1995, page 3.*

13. *Greg Ogden.* Discipleship Essentials: A Guide to Building Your Life in Christ. *Downers Grove, Illinois: Intervarsity Press, 1998, page 21.*

14. *Alvin Christopher Bernstine.* How to Develop a Department of Christian Education within the Local Baptist Church: A Congregational Enablement Model. *Nashville: Townsend Press, 1995, page 99.*

EQUIPPING THE SAINTS
FOR SERVICE

The Goals of Christian Education in the African American Church

Simply put, the task of Christian education is to educate and equip Christians with the tools for effective Bible study and transferable Christian principles for application in their daily lives.[1]

TO BE EFFECTIVE, CHRISTIAN EDUCATION REQUIRES THE COMMITMENT of the entire church—pastors and lay leaders, ministry participants, and members of all ages—to an intentional program of learning about and for Christ. Christian discipleship, like learning, is a lifelong process requiring commitment to taking in new information, placing it in the context of one's life, and applying its principles on a routine basis.

Like secular education, Christian education is guided by a set of assumptions about learners, those qualified to teach, and the value of the subject matter being presented. Unlike secular education, Christian education is ultimately soul-saving: Its learners include its teachers, it is of the highest possible value to the individual and the community of believers, and it has in it the seeds of redemption.

Assumptions Guiding Christian Education

Christian education teaches a set of underlying Christian values. The fundamental assumptions of Christian education and Christian educators[2] are that:

People are of ultimate worth. Jesus views each individual as worthy and important. As the song states, "His eye is on the sparrow and I know he watches me." Jesus came to save us (John 3:17), spending much of his ministry working with people considered to be social outcasts. Christian education provides informational opportunities for learning the expectations of discipleship, understanding the life and teachings of Jesus, and determining the spiritual gifts that each Christian can contribute to the community of believers. Because Christ values each of us, one responsibility of Christian educators is to provide settings where all who seek to know Christ feel accepted.

Humanity exists in a fallen state. The fall of humanity began in the Garden of Eden. Through their willing disobedience to God, Adam and Eve alienated themselves from God and from the purpose for which he had created them (Genesis 3) and, as their descendents, placed all of humankind in a fallen state. One important goal of the Christian church is to return believers to right relationship with God. If, as the elders say, the church is a hospital for sinners rather than a society of saints, Christian educators are in a position to work with church members regardless of their spiritual state. In addition to training that facilitates their ability to share fundamental religious education with church members, Christian educators must be kind and compassionate people who model Christian lives.

Jesus Christ provides total salvation for humanity. Christians are redeemed, saved, by Christ's sacrifice on the cross (Romans 5:8-11). "Christian educators must view the saving work of Jesus Christ as an essential dynamic of Christian education. In fact, it is the saving work of Jesus Christ which shapes the goals of Christian education."[3] Christian educators are called upon to recognize that there are no persons or situations beyond Christ's saving capacity and to incorporate this knowledge into their curriculum and teaching.

The church represents Jesus Christ in the world. Jesus came to earth to save us and to deliver us from our lives of sin by making for us the ultimate sacrifice of his life. He asked us to be his witnesses, carrying his work and his Word throughout the whole world (Acts 1:8). The organized church, therefore, represents Jesus Christ in the world. Christian educators have the awesome responsibility of assisting in the training of disciples who are well equipped for their roles as representatives of Christ on earth.

The church equips people to equip others for faithful service. The Great Commission commands us to go into all of the world, teaching the goodness of God, proclaiming Christ's role as our Lord and Savior and bringing new souls to Christ (Mark 16:15). Christian education helps to create disciples who are sufficiently knowledgeable to engage in this Christian responsibility. Christian educators educate others to teach the lessons of Christ.

Christian education is the church's primary equipping ministry. Equipping the saints for service occurs through worship, prayer meetings, personal spiritual reflection, a broad range of church activities, and the offerings of departments of Christian education. "The specific assignment of Christian education is to provide the church with a ministry that facilitates the disciple-making process. It is through the ministry of Christian education that persons are enabled to be 'the church.'"[4] In coordination with the other ministries of the church, Christian educators provide a fertile spiritual and informational foundation for church members.

The Purpose of Christian Education

The purpose of Christian education is to help Christians lay personal and corporate foundations for service to Christ, equipping us with the information we require to:

- Learn basic Christian beliefs (**theology**)
- Gain knowledge about the life of Jesus
- Understand and commit ourselves to the study of the Bible
- Become disciples of Christ
- Increase awareness of the history of the Christian church
- Learn God's plan for our lives
- Prepare ourselves for change
- Create a community of Christian believers
- Incorporate into our lives the beliefs and expectations of Christianity
- Participate fully in the ritual of worship
- Identify and appropriately use spiritual gifts
- Discern the commitment of Christianity
- Become good stewards of the resources that God has given us

- Learn the history and specific beliefs of our denominations
- Grow toward maturity in Christ
- Remake our lives to God's purpose
- Be prepared for faithful service
- Grow in our understanding of God's Word and his will for the world and our individual lives

---

TEACHABLE MOMENT

The purpose of Christian education is to effectively educate the Christian community to duplicate disciples and to make a lifetime commitment to grow intimately with the Trinity.

Rev. Barbara Peacock, Minister of Discipleship, University Park Baptist Church, e-mail interview, August 28, 2002

Because much of our educational focus centers on the teaching of basic theology, Dr. Forrest Harris offers the following theological statements as launching pads for reflection on the meaning of Christian faith and the importance of Christian education:

- The content of God's revelation is salvation and liberation
- The primary record of that salvation is the Bible
- A God who loves, liberates, and saves is revealed in the Bible
- God's self-revelation is Jesus Christ, liberator and mediator of human salvation
- Jesus Christ embodies human sufferings in such a way that all people can know God's love, justice, reconciliation, and freedom, and be liberated to share in a community of faith
- Communities of faith are given the power of the Holy Spirit to be agents of God's love and freedom in the world[5]

Because it is such a fundamental ministry of the church, Christian education must be more than the transfer of knowledge from Christian educators to church members. Its design and its teachers must be undergirded by Christian theology, strong philosophies of education, and extensive teacher training and preparation. As a tool for aiding in the building of Christ's church, the theory and practice of Christian education must take into account its ultimate purpose.

The Purpose of Christian Education in the African American Context

African-centered Christian education adheres to the goals and purposes of Christian education in general, but adds some important and distinctive considerations:

Correcting history. Many African Americans feel called upon to defend Christianity against claims that it is the "white man's religion." There exist, however, significant data that indicate the early movement of Christianity into northern and southern portions of Africa. Slaves brought to America, even though most were not Christian, were easily able to accept Christianity because of a shared belief in a supreme being, the similarity of traditions (full immersion baptism, for example, resembles the customs of West African river cults), and an understanding that "as a Black oppressed people, facing daily the White oppressor, the Exodus took on a political as well as a religious meaning."[6]

Meeting needs specific to the survival and advancement of African Americans. African Americans continue to have a number of survival needs that are reflected in our struggles for social equity. African American churches have traditionally developed ministries that focus on providing for the least, the lost, and the last among us but are increasingly called upon to address current and often troubling social problems such as drug addiction, single parenthood, inadequate educational opportunities and performance, and community health issues such as diabetes, prostate cancer, HIV/AIDS, and other health-related problems that disproportionately affect African Americans. Survival is, of course, greatly aided by church community support, acknowledgment, and celebration of our triumphs and successes in all areas of personal, family, and group endeavor. African American churches are adept at celebrating our achievements by posting photographic displays or having as speakers or honored guests men and women who have broken barriers and succeeded in venues previously closed to us, and those who have excelled in places where the doors have been open a bit longer. In addition, African American churches celebrate the achievements of their congregants, with ceremonial observances of educational milestones, awards, and wedding anniversaries.

Re-establishing important cultural values. African and African American values have traditionally reflected the strengths of our communities. In recent context, those strengths have been reconstituted both by our culture and the majority culture as negatives. It must therefore be the role of the African American church to reinvigorate its teachings with the positive beliefs and standards that have supported us and aided our survival. Incorporation of the principles of Nguza Saba found in the Kwaanza celebration are but one way that African American churches infuse traditional Africentric beliefs into Christian education. (See Teachable Moment on page 19.)

Christian Education as a Tool for the Soul's Liberation

An interesting way to think about the purpose of Christian education is as a tool for liberation, specifically, our liberation from sin to salvation. Though he was not a religious educator, the ideas of Brazilian educator Paulo Freire (1921–1997) were informed by Christianity. Especially popular in Africa, Asia, and Latin America, Freire is the most well known thinker on effective ways to teach people who have been oppressed.

In Eurocentric models of thought, liberation is often considered a "gift," something given to an oppressed people by a thoughtful (but superior) society. Freire created a revolution in educational thinking by proposing that liberation and education were equivalent and mutual processes. In other words, education is necessary for the liberation of communities of oppressed people, *and* education and liberation are partnerships that must work together for the good of all communities. Freire's work focuses on:

- **Popular** and **informal education**, ways of creating a community of learners through methods that encourage dialogue (rather than relying on strict direction from a curriculum),[7] and

TEACHABLE MOMENT

The Seven Principles of Nguzo Saba

I.   UMOJA (UNITY)
     (oo-MOE-jah). To strive for and maintain unity in the family, com-
     munity, nation, and race.

II. KUJICHAGULIA (SELF DETERMINATION)
     (koo-jee-cha-goo-LEE-ah). To define ourselves, name ourselves,
     create for ourselves, and speak for ourselves.

III. UJIMA (COLLECTIVE WORK AND RESPONSIBILITY)
     (oo-JEE-mah). To build and maintain our community together and
     to make our brothers' and sisters' problems our problems and to
     solve them together.

IV. UJAMAA (COOPERATIVE ECONOMICS)
     (oo-JAH-mah). To build and maintain our own stores, shops, and
     other businesses and to profit together from them.

V.   NIA (PURPOSE)
     (nee-AH). To make as our collective vocation the building and
     developing of our community in order to restore our people to
     their traditional greatness.

VI. KUUMBA (CREATIVITY)
     (koo-OOM-bah). To do always as much as we can, in the way
     that we can, in order to leave our community more beautiful and
     beneficial than when we inherited it.

VII. IMANI (FAITH)
     (ee-MAH-nee). To believe with all our hearts in our parents, our
     teachers, our leaders, our people, and the righteousness and vic-
     tory of our struggle.

www.geocities.com, keyword: Kwaanza, accessed September 6, 2002

- Creating a **community of learners.** Informal education assumes that teacher and student are flexible roles where learning occurs through discussions. In these discussions the contributions of each community member are equally valued. Informal education does not use the more formal European strategy of educational **banking** in which the teacher makes "deposits of knowledge" in the student.

Freire focused on five strategies for educating people who have been oppressed, people who have not often had a voice in determining their destinies:

1. **Dialogue.** Dialogue is conversation through which learning occurs in an environment that respects all ideas. It does not involve one person teaching another person. Instead, dialogue requires a community of learners who work together to understand an issue and to apply that information to their lives.

   - *Note to Christian educators:* Often Christian educators give lectures to their students, sharing their knowledge about the Bible and engaging in the traditional educational practice of **banking** (depositing information into students). Instead, Freire recommends that the best educational method for liberation is "problem-posing," posing problems that students work together to solve.

   - *Challenge to Christian educators:* Provide opportunities for learning based on the contributions of each member of the class. While the teacher may possess knowledge that is new to students, the class should be structured so that students have open discussions about Christian beliefs and history, biblical history, the application of Christian beliefs to their lives, and beliefs specific to their **denomination.** (See Section Three for information about teaching strategies for different age groups and populations of students).

2. **Praxis. Praxis** is action that is informed by and linked to shared values. In Freire's model, dialogue is not just about conversation. It is a strategy for making a difference in the world through relationships based on shared values. That difference is made through creating and supporting the needs of a community of learners whose questions and ideas are viewed as vital and important. By valuing

all learners, we create opportunities for human beings to flourish and, in turn, to share their gifts with the larger community.

- *Note to Christian educators:* Christianity is concerned with a very clear set of shared values.
- *Challenge to Christian educators:* Shared Christian values are communicated to others, inside and outside the church, through our actions. As leaders in the church we must be aware that others are looking to us as examples. Christian educators must be careful to "walk the talk," living lives that are examples of their beliefs.

3. **Conscientization.** Conscientization is a complicated term for developing a conscience about the world. Because of his faith in the liberating power of education, Freire believed that those freed by education have a responsibility to create similar opportunities for others.

- *Note to Christian educators:* **Evangelism** is one method of developing a conscience about the world. Effective evangelizing requires understanding the communities that are entered to share information about Christ.
- *Challenge to Christian educators:* Denominations often have different beliefs about the role of the church in addressing social issues. However, Freire's ideas have direct application to sharing the love of Jesus with others through the use of dialogue (teaching and preaching) and evangelism.

4. **Experience.** Informal education is most effective when participants share their experiences with one another. Freire believed in the power of personal stories as tools for informal education and for creating a community of learners.

- *Note to Christian educators:* In all Christian education venues, participants (teachers, students, and congregants) can be called on to share their experiences and to place them within the context of Christian beliefs.
- *Challenge to Christian educators:* Provide opportunities for students and congregants to share their experiences of Christ with one another. This can occur through testimonials and prayer, in class discussions, in evangelizing activities, through

dramatic presentation and artistic projects, and by shared worship experiences.

5. **Christian references.** Freire was influenced in his thinking by the sacrifice of Jesus for his followers. He felt that, like Christ, teachers must also be sacrificial. In his view, teachers must release traditional educational ideas and formats that hinder liberation, so that they can develop a community of learners. In that community, teachers share dialogues and experiences that free oppressed people, helping them develop tools that create positive actions that can assist their local communities and the surrounding world. (See Chapter One for Dr. Forrest Harris's discussion of the liberating qualities of Christianity.)

- *Note to Christian educators:* According to one of Freire's students, "An educator is a person who has to live in the deep significance of Easter."[8]
- *Challenge to Christian educators:* Maintaining a personal relationship with Easter means keeping Christ's sacrifice and divinity at the forefront of our thoughts.

Being Prepared to Teach

Once sure of the responsibilities, goals, and purpose of Christian education, one must be prepared to teach.

Shortly after his appointment as a professor of music at the University of California, Los Angeles, [Jascha] Heifitz was asked what had prompted this change in direction in his career.[9] "Violin playing is a perishable art," said Heifitz solemnly. "It must be passed on as a personal skill; otherwise it is lost." Then, with a smile, he continued: "I remember my old violin professor in Russia. He said that someday I would be good enough to teach."[10]

Though the Word of God is not perishable, Christian education is an art that is built upon faith and that occurs within the context of personal relationships within the church. Christian educators must assess their skills and purpose in sharing information that encourages believers and brings them closer to Christ. Christian educators must create relationships that facilitate learning in their congregations. They must support active dialogue, explore shared values, develop student interest in and contributions to the world outside the church, and help students use their experiences to connect meaningfully to the Word of God. Christian educators, too, must be good enough to teach.

Notes

1. *Rev. Tonya Burton, Minister of Discipleship, Metropolitan Baptist Church, Washington, D.C.* Interview, *July 10, 2002.*

2. *Assumptions in bold typeface are found in Alvin Christopher Bernstine.* How to Develop a Department of Christian Education within the Local Baptist Church: A Congregational Enablement Model. *Nashville: Townsend Press, 1995, pages 10–13. Unless otherwise noted, the commentaries following the assumptions are written by the author.*

3. *Bernstine.* How to Develop a Department of Christian Education within the Local Baptist Church, *page 11.*

4. *Bernstine.* How to Develop a Department of Christian Education within the Local Baptist Church, *page 13.*

5. *Dr. Forrest Harris.* Theology from a Black Baptist Perspective. *Seminar VI, Ministers' Division of the National Baptist Congress of Christian Education, St. Louis, Missouri, June 17–21, 2002, pages 131–132.*

6. *Latta R. Thomas, quoted by J. Deotis Roberts.* Africentric Christianity: A Theological Appraisal for Ministry. *Valley Forge: Judson Press, 2000, page 47.*

7. *It is important to understand that Freire was not anti-curriculum. He wanted all methods of teaching to be informed by the learners so that educational processes reflected an equal relationship between "teachers" and "students." For Freire, curriculum development is a community process that assesses needs and provides information that meets them.*

8. *Paul Taylor.* The Texts of Freire. *Buckingham: Open University Press, 1993, page 53.*

9. *Heifitz is considered one of the greatest violinists in modern history.*

10. *Clifton Fadimon, general editor.* The Little, Brown Book of Anecdotes. *Boston: Little, Brown, 1985, page 5.*

CHAPTER THREE

BECOMING IN CHRIST

Traditions of Christian Teaching

Teach me, O LORD, to follow your decrees; then I will
keep them to the end (Psalm 119:33).

BECOMING GOOD ENOUGH TO TEACH REQUIRES PREPARATION. Christian education is a method for encouraging active scholarship among those interested in learning about and living for Jesus. Christian education requires Christian approaches, strategies built on "instructional methods [that] reflect in great measure your concept of how the human mind works and how we learn [your **epistemology**]. As Christian educators we need to use those instructional methods that will most effectively help our learners incorporate the truths of God's self-revelation into their minds and hearts."[1]

Building on the traditional education theory, Christian education provides instruction to teach theology, share essential religious information (Christian and denominational), impart a Christian framework with which to interpret learned material, and encourage the generalization of Christian learning outside of the classroom. African American Christian educators often focus on an additional set of teaching imperatives: to incorporate into shared Christian information an acknowledgment of our cultural history and current situation—the African-ness of Jesus; the role of Christ's grace, goodness, and mercy in "how we got over"; and of our continued struggles—and the establishment of a supportive environment in which the African American church can thrive as an extended family, as children of God, richly and variously colored ("Have we not all one Father?" Malachi 2:10) who are prepared to "carry each other's burdens" (Galatians 6:2).

Christian education ascribes to a broad range of assumptions about what Christians require in order to be well trained for service to Christ.

Christian educators are vital, therefore, to the mission of the church. To be prepared for this important and necessary task of the church, Christian educators, both professional and volunteer teachers, are called to understand the enormity of their commitment to the life of the local church and its role in the church of God.

Assumptions about Christian Teaching and Christian Teachers

"The demands of Christian teaching never prove to be easy. Our mandates of evangelism and discipleship demand the use of maximally effective methods. Maturity in this vocation of teaching (professional and volunteer) is evidenced by the increased availability on the part of the teacher to facilitate a learning process that brings out the creative uniqueness with which God invested each learner. This is essentially the art of teaching."[2]

Noting that Christian educators must be dedicated to personal growth in Christ, Israel Galindo, author of *The Craft of Christian Teaching*, describes three assumptions that underlie their spiritual role[3]:

1. **The Holy Spirit is active in the teacher-learner relationship.** Christian educators must be guided by the hand of God. They must understand that teaching is more than the words that emerge from the mouth of the teacher. Students, Christians seeking information and guidance, pay attention to what is said and how it is said by those responsible for their instruction. While no one expects perfection from any Christian, it is our goal to strive to be Christ-like. When Christian educators engage publicly in negative behaviors or use their classrooms to act out personal issues, they interfere significantly with the Christian learning process.

2. **Christian learning is a lifelong process.** Teachers teach and teachers learn. Christian educators must be committed to their continued personal growth. Christian educators must engage in personal study, take classes, and seek guidance that allows them to grow as Christians. As a result of this commitment, Christian educators grow in their walk with Christ and increase the informational pool and strategic tools that can make them better teachers. Conversely,

students learn and students teach. By using new information as a guide for interpreting personal experience, Christian education students teach others how the hand of God becomes manifest in their lives.

3. **Christian teaching is uniquely different from other ways of teaching.** Its goals and aims, previously described, are evangelistic and are driven by the demand to create disciples. As in all forms of teaching, there are immutable facts, there is controversy, and there is mystery. Christian teaching presents facts (the teachings of Christ as set forth in the Bible and, most particularly, in the New Testament), provides a framework for understanding those facts (Christ's expectations of Christians and strategies for using Christianity as the focus of successful living in a challenging world), addresses controversy, frequently from a perspective forwarded by the denominational interpretation of Scripture, and revels in the mystery of Christ. Finally, Christian education differs from other forms of education in its soul-liberating qualities.[4] As is noted in 2 Chronicles 7:14, "If my people, who are called by my name, will humble themselves and pray and seek my face and turn from their wicked ways, then will I hear from heaven and will forgive their sin and will heal their land."

TEACHABLE MOMENT

"A functioning department of Christian education awards qualitative honor to any congregation which embraces the honorable mission of Christian education. The local church which prioritizes Christian education leaps in the direction of quality fulfillment of the Christian mission. It is without question that the Lord expects us to do our best; and we can do our best, give our best, and be our best only when we know what is best."

Alvin Christopher Bernstine. *How to Develop a Department of Christian Education within the Local Baptist Church: A Congregational Enablement Model.* Nashville: Townsend Press, 1995, page 1

Eurocentric Approaches to Christian Education

In 1933, Carter G. Woodson wrote a book titled *The Miseducation of the Negro,* a title that referenced the teaching traditions that the oppressor uses to inform the oppressed. "The so-called modern education with all its defects, however, does others so much more good than it does the Negro, because it has been worked out in conformity to the needs of those who have enslaved and oppressed weaker peoples."[5] A modern student of educational inequalities sees Woodson's concerns as unfortunately current. "One of the most important challenges we face as a people, is to continue our efforts at offsetting our continued miseducation of the contributions of African people from ancient times to the present in all subjects—such as mathematics, science, social studies, language arts, art, and music."[6] Part of the role of African American Christian educators is to correct miseducation regarding Afri-Christian history so that parishioners are well informed about their history of Christian praise.

Traditional Eurocentric educational approaches to Christian education use the model of secular education to provide instructional strategies. However, the teaching strategies used in Christian education have several potential problems. These strategies are:

- inattentive to the learning styles and needs of Christian education students
- focused on Christ from a Eurocentric perspective
- not used to re-educate African Americans about the roles of blacks in Christian history, even when they may otherwise be Africentric in their approach

Christian education classes often focus on outmoded methods as well as strategies that do not address the different learning styles and needs that may be present in any Christian education venue. Christian education classes, for example, often use a lecture format for students of a variety of ages and call for the recitation of materials learned through rote memorization.

Think about Sunday school classes you were involved in as a child. Remember the teachers who would remind you of a Bible story, then present sentences for which you had to fill in the blank? The teacher might have said, "And the angel of the Lord told the shepherds that they would find the baby in what?[7] And lying where?"[8] While this teaching method is designed to develop an understanding of the Christmas story, it facilitates unnecessary "wrong" answers[9] and actually limits understanding by stifling discussion.

Now, walk into a Sunday school class next Sunday. In many classes you will find the same old methodology, teaching strategies that children tolerate until their parents can no longer force them to go to Sunday school. Walk into many adult Christian education classes and you will see something similarly stifling—well-meaning Christian teachers preaching at their adult students, holding forth with long soliloquies that serve as evidence of teacher knowledge but do little to engage sustained interest or long-term retention of information.

One of my worst Christian education experiences involved a class on the Old Testament where a particular passage, which I can no longer remember, used a number of different names for God. There was a capital "G" God and a small "g" god and a reference to Yahweh. I asked the teacher, a young minister, to explain to me and to the class the different terms for God in this passage and their importance to the period of biblical history we were studying. "Was the small "g" a reference to idols?" I asked. "Did the presence of God and Yahweh in the same passage of Scripture represent a transition from one view of God to another? And if so, what historical events spurred the changing perception of God among those people at that time during the eras represented by the Old Testament?" I was a thoughtful student, one who was trying to make sense of what I was reading so that I could understand how God moved through history. This was the minister's response: "God is God and that's all you need to know." As you might imagine, no other substantive questions were asked for the rest of the class. It was probably the case that the young minister simply did not know how to respond, which is fine. I willingly acknowledge that I am a challenging and occasionally overly curious student. However, other class participants may have had enough information from their personal Bible study to create a rich dialogue based on my questions. But no such dialogue happened. The teacher preached at us and lectured us, and the students, all adults, alternately took notes and tuned out. I stopped attending the class. It was clear to me that there was not sufficient respect for my learning needs and interests. This teacher was stuck on old methods, was inadequately prepared for the subject matter that was planned for that week, discouraged those who genuinely wanted to learn, and, unwilling to admit to a lack of knowledge, stopped what could have been an interesting and informative discourse.

Knowing yourself as a Christian educator means giving yourself permission to be a learner as well as a teacher. We cannot know everything. We aren't expected to. That's why there is not only one of us on the planet. That is why we were given the gift of learning in the context of a Christian community. Christian educators must feel comfortable saying, "That is a wonderful question, one for which I don't have a clear answer at the moment. Let's think this through together. Does anyone in the class want to try to answer the question?" Or, "That is a good question, and I will do some research to try to provide an informed answer the next time we meet. In fact, let's all do some research and take this on as next week's lesson."

In the past thirty years, and most especially in the last ten, secular educational methodologies have made significant shifts in the strategies that are available to teachers and that are essential for those who wish to be excellent teachers. Christian education, a form of teaching that occurs within a community of faith that seeks greater knowledge of Christ for the purposes of evangelism and the making of disciples, can greatly benefit from attention to learning styles, developmental differences in learning, and an array of teaching methods to make every component of Christian education a vibrant, exciting, and meaningful experience.

Traditional Teaching versus Christian Education

The goal-based differences between traditional secular teaching and Christian education should be sufficient to make Christian teaching innovative and distinctive. As noted in Chapter Two, Christian education seeks to provide the information that allows believers to fulfill their responsibility for effective discipleship, evangelism, and kingdom building. For this reason, effective Christian education programs build a community of supportive believers who share values, walk similar paths, and seek individual and corporate growth in Christ as a lifelong and eternal goal.

The following table[10] notes significant focal differences between schooling and Christian education:

Table 1

	Traditional Schooling	Christian Education
CONTEXT	School or classroom	Community of faith
CONTENT	Text or creed	Person of Jesus Christ
APPROACH	Didactic or instructional	Relational
OUTCOME	Mastery of content	Becoming while in relationship
METHODS	Schooling or laboratory	Relational

The example of the minister-teacher provided in the story above reflects someone who used a traditional schooling model, was **didactic** (though not effectively so) in his approach, appeared to be confused about the goals and purpose of Christian education, and was not aware of the power inherent in the relational aspects of learning. Freire would say that this minister-teacher was focused on banking information into his students rather than using the problem-posing method of liberating discussion. This minister-teacher's approach to teaching the Old Testament overused lecture and denied the opportunity for questions that facilitated the application of learning to the lives of class participants. If, as Galindo notes, effective Christian education builds an intentional relationship in a community of faith that is based on the life, teachings, and love of Christ, then it must be engaged in as more than a commitment of heart and belief. Christian educators must view their work as craft, as art honed for Christ's glory.

Christian Education as a Creative Craft

Christian education is a vocation, a calling, a commitment, and a craft. As with all talents, Christian educators must hone their skills so that they become excellent teachers, capable of providing enriching environments for Christian learners. Excellent Christian educators:

Prepare themselves for teaching. They use all resources available to them (independent research, teacher training classes, observation of other teachers) to determine the teaching styles and strategies most likely to be useful with their students.

Practice what they teach. As part of their preparation for teaching, Christian educators must know themselves, especially their motivations for teaching and their preferred learning style. They must be well trained to work in a Christian setting, availing themselves of all accessible resources. Practicing what we preach also means living Christian lives.

Treat each class as a new experience. While teaching experience is invaluable in achieving comfort in teaching and in perfecting the craft of teaching, each new class should provide a new experience and challenge for Christian educators. "Canned presentations," repeated like tape recordings class after class, are a sign that teachers are not developing relationships with their students that can be used to guide class discussions, fuel research into current topics and events that might be informed by a Christian perspective, or create a comfortable flow in a room full of motivated and interested learners.

Understand principles of learning. It is essential that Christian educators understand that people learn in different ways. Some are visual learners; others learn best through auditory methods. Yet other learners are kinesthetic in their approach, requiring teaching styles that allow them to interact with people and materials. Though educators may themselves have a preferred manner of learning, their classrooms must address the learning needs of all types of learners. Additionally, persons at different developmental stages (early and later childhood, teen years, young and older adults) need specific teaching adaptations so that they remain engaged, interested, and motivated learners. While I feel that it is a sin to teach anyone poorly, the sin is compounded when Christian educators do not take learning theory into account and run the risk of turning off minds that should be attuned to God's Word and its meaning for them and the community of Christian believers. See Section Two for information on learning styles and teaching strategies appropriate for different developmental levels.

Are adept at using prepared and original materials. Christian educators, adept at their craft, make learning exciting. They excite in Christian learners a desire to understand the Word of God and apply it in meaningful ways to their own lives. Expert Christian educators learn to present all materials as if they are original. Not depending on a word-for-word replay of written materials, they ask questions likely to encourage thoughtful discussions, use real-life examples that class participants can relate to, and pay attention to individual and group learning styles and informational needs. By recognizing the learning needs of each classroom, Christian educators can also determine what adaptations should be made to increase the relevance and long-term impact of their classes.

Alter the "W sequence." Many educators, Christian and secular, get stuck on the W questions—who, what, when, where, why, and, occasionally, how. The most effective questions for creating discussions that focus on how materials are interpreted, rather than on rote memorization, ask "why", "what", "if" ("if" questions force comparisons of information), "suppose..." (questions that use suppositions ask learners to use their imaginations), and "imagine that..." (this type of question puts learners in someone else's position, causing them to examine personal values and beliefs).

Celebrate the "aha" experience. Learning is a journey of discovery. Learning in a Christian context is also a celebratory experience, one in which new and established Christians can continually find information that supports their experience of the movement of God in their lives. Sharing these experiences enhances the growth of each individual participant in Christian education classes and strengthens the Christian community.

Share Afri-Christian history. All African American Christians should be able to defend our faith, a task that involves knowledge of the roles that Africans play in the Bible and in early Christian missions, the similarities and differences between ancient African religious traditions and Christianity, the role of Christianity as a solace during slavery, the giants of African American Christian history, and the history of African American churches.

Effective Christian teaching is exciting for the teacher and the learner. "There's nothing quite like watching a master craftsperson at work. A teacher who is good at craft inspires learning. The craft of teaching includes knowing how to ask questions, how to motivate students, how to use educational technologies, how to lead a dialogue, how to prepare audiovisuals, how to 'read' a group, how to plan a lesson, how to discipline and how to give praise, and how to model behavior and attitudes. And it includes knowing when to speak and when not to speak, when to give a little and when to push, even how to wipe a runny nose, and how to keep chalk dust off your dark blue suit."[11] African-centered Christian education is especially exciting because it is more than excellent craft: it is a way of reclaiming history, teaching truth, and contributing to corrective education within religious and other contexts.

Notes

1. *Israel Galindo*. The Craft of Christian Teaching: Essentials for Becoming a Very Good Teacher. *Valley Forge, Judson Press, 1998, page 19.*
2. *Galindo*, The Craft of Christian Teaching, *page 22.*
3. *Galindo*. The Craft of Christian Teaching, *page x. Assumptions in bold are Galindo's; commentary is the author's.*
4. *Freire, for example, discussed education's impact on intellectual and social liberation.*
5. *Carter G. Woodson in Dr. Conrad W. Worrell's article entitled "Breaking the Miseducation Cycle." www.ascac.org (www.google.com, keyword: miseducation of the Negro), accessed September 6, 2002.*
6. *Worrell, "Breaking the Miseducation Cycle," www.ascac.org, accessed September 6, 2002.*
7. *Swaddling clothes.*
8. *A manger.*
9. *The first question is intended to ask what Jesus was wearing, but it could be understood as a question about* where *he was—in a manger.*
10. *Galindo*, The Craft of Christian Teaching, *page 18.*
11. *Galindo*, The Craft of Christian Teaching, *pages 77–78.*

WOULDN'T TAKE NOTHING FOR MY JOURNEY

Christian Education in the African American Context

Oh God, grant us understanding
To know ourselves,
As the legitimate heirs
To the rich land of Africa.[1]

HISTORICALLY, AFRICAN AMERICAN CHURCHES HAVE ALWAYS BEEN educational institutions. While the different black denominations vary in their educational programs and approaches, in all of our churches education has long been positively acknowledged for its capacity to equalize social and economic inequities. In the early AME church, for example, "the church leaders were not educated people, but they had a clear perception of what education would mean to the interests of the church and the advancement of the African people then held in abject slavery. Bishop Daniel Payne, who had been a schoolmaster in Baltimore, set the educational goals for the fledgling institution by insisting upon a trained ministry, and by encouraging AME pastors to organize schools in their communities as an aspect of their ministries."[2]

Seen as a tool for removing the social and emotional shackles of bondage, educational opportunity in its secular and Christian forms provides for African Americans something that cannot be stolen from us: minds tuned to knowledge and prepared for excellence. When public education has failed to provide for our children learning experiences that are rich and meaningful, we have responded through social protest, lawsuits and legislation, and by developing church-sponsored Christian schools. Although new generations of African Americans, uneducated about their history, correlate educational

excellence with "whiteness," the church has most often been supportive of education as a laudable goal for strengthening the African American community.[3]

TEACHABLE MOMENT

Generations for Christ

The psalmist exhorted the Israelites to teach their children about God
and his statutes so that future generations would remain faithful to
the Lord. When a generation of people is ignorant of God, they have
no moral bearings and seek spiritual experience and truth in the
wrong people. That is why it is required of all Christians to provide
younger generations of Christians with training and guidance.

Echoes: Teaching God's Resounding Word. Adult Comprehensive
Bible Study of the Progressive National Baptist Convention, Inc.,
June, July, August 2002. Lesson from June 30, 2002, page 39

Christian Education in the African American Context

African American Christian education is called upon to re-educate us
about our role in Christian history, the nature of our faith, and the
broadness of our spiritual traditions. "The spirituality of black theology arises out of the experiences of social change and traditions found
in several stories—the radical calling in the Christian Bible, African
American women's spirituality, and the folk faith of enslaved black
workers. Just as the God of freedom incarnated God's self in the birth,
life, crucifixion, and resurrection of Jesus the Liberator, so, too, God's
same spirit of freedom incarnates itself among poor African Americans suffering in life threatening situations and crying out in their
struggle for a productive and complete life."[4] Christian education in
the African American context teaches the importance of such stories
in their historical and current contexts.

In our churches, Christian education has also been used to provide a supplemental form of traditional schooling (Christian

schools) as well as to engage the mandates of the Great Commission through teaching that is focused on Scripture (Sunday school, Vacation Bible School, prayer meeting, worship and topical Christian education classes) and that reflects African and African American history and circumstances.

African American Christian religious expression often reflects our struggle for justice, equality, and freedom in America. In his book, *Black Culture and Black Consciousness*, Lawrence W. Levine notes the ways that American blacks have connected their experience of oppression with their faith: "Upon the hard rock of racial, social, and economic exploitation and injustice, black Americans forged and nurtured a culture: they formed and maintained kinship networks, raised and socialized children, built a religion, and created a rich expressive culture in which they articulated their feelings and hopes and dreams."[5]

TEACHABLE MOMENT

Because of the unique history of African Americans, specific lessons are taught (in our Christian education program) which focus on the Bible as a book that tells the story of an African people. The goal is to help members to heal from the de-humanization of a racist experience by seeing that God has always had something to do with us, and to identify with the redemption drama.

Rev. James Perkins, Pastor, Greater Christ Baptist Church, Detroit, Michigan, telephone interview, August 5, 2002

Robert M. Franklin identifies specific traditions of African American spirituality that are evident in our religious practice. (See Table 2.) Using a holistic definition of Christian education as occurring in all of the activities of the church, the African American religious context is attuned to these roles of the church: evangelical, holy, charismatic, social justice oriented, Africentric, and contemplative. In recognition that many people now choose to experience their spirituality outside

Table 2[6]

Spirituality Tradition	Spiritual End	Spiritual Discipline	Spiritual Exemplar
Evangelical	Knowledge of God's Word	Teaching, preaching, and study	William Bentley
Holiness	Purity of life and thought	Fasting, prayer, and renunciation	Arenia C. Mallory
Charismatic	Empowerment through the Spirit	Tarrying, seeking spiritual gifts	William J. Seymour
Social Justice	Public righteousness	Community activism, political activity	Vernon Johns
Afrocentric	Celebration of black identity	Cultural displays of African heritage	George Alexander McGuire
Contemplative	Intimacy with God	Prayer, meditation	Howard Thurman
New Age	Peace of mind	Meditation, chanting, music	Dionne Warwick

of traditional religion, Franklin includes a category labeled "New Age" that combines Eastern and Western philosophies and spiritual practices. Noting that each form of spiritual practice has an expected format (spiritual discipline) and outcome (spiritual end), Franklin describes a number of processes, each of which can be considered a form of teaching, as well as a teacher (exemplar) whose body of work can be used as a reference.

Christian education has at its disposal a wide variety of tools—prayer, preaching, fasting, teaching, activism, and service—to help new and established believers understand God's Word and Christian expectations and commitments. Christian education should be a transforming experience, one that allows learners to thoughtfully access God's Word, become empowered through the presence of the Holy Spirit, celebrate ethnic and racial culture, and serve Christ by serving others. Christian education provides tools for that service.

African-Centered Strategies for Christian Education

Black congregations, formed under the leadership of powerful black preachers like George Liele and Andrew Bryan, began the work of saving souls in the 1780s. Independent African American denominations, seven in all, were founded to assure that the doors of the church were open to all. African-centered Christian education teaches our particular history as Christians through a directed focus on the:

Development of African-centered Christian Values. The values of African American churches must be reflected in the mission and vision of the local church, infused into all worship experiences and programmatic content, and demonstrated in behavior. On the walls of the church and in all written materials produced by Trinity United Church of Christ, an African centered church in a predominantly white denomination, values are evident. Trinity's Black Value System, adopted in 1981, includes twelve precepts (see details in Chapter Fourteen). Their vision, which also reflects their values, calls on the congregation to make a set of specific commitments that actively engage them in work on behalf of their and other communities in the building of God's kingdom on earth. The vision for the congregation for the first decade of the twenty-first century is:

- A congregation committed to Adoration.
- A congregation preaching Salvation.
- A congregation actively seeking Reconcilliation.
- A congregation with a non-negotiable Commitment to Africa.
- A congregation committed to Biblical Education.
- A congregation committed to Cultural Education.
- A congregation committed to the Historical Education of African People in the Diaspora.

- A congregation committed to Liberation.
- A congregation committed to Restoration.
- A congregation committed to Economic Parity.

History of the African American Church. The African American denominations—African Methodist Episcopal (AME), African Methodist Episcopal Zion (AME Zion), Baptists [in the National Baptist Convention USA, Inc. (NBC)], National Baptist Convention of America (NBCA) and Progressive National Baptist Convention (PNBC), Christian (originally Colored) Methodist Episcopal (CME), and the Church of God in Christ (COGIC)—each have unique histories of service to the souls of their congregants. These histories should be taught to the members of each denomination as part of new members training. The broader history of African American denominational traditions is another form of education that provides parishioners with an understanding of the similarities and differences in our faith traditions.

Understanding our history and African-centered Christian theology. African American Christians benefit greatly from learning about Africans in the Bible. Africans in the Old Testament include Asenath (Genesis 41, 46), Shiphrah (Exodus 1), Puah (Genesis 46, Exodus 1), Jethro (Exodus 3, 4, 18), Zipporah (Exodus 2, 4, 18) and Ebed-Melech (Jeremiah 38). Those in the New Testament are Jesus, Peter, Paul, and the Ethiopian eunuch (Acts 8).[7] Learning that Jesus is black is news to many African Americans. Our theology understandably shifts, however, when we understand that our history as Christians began with Christ, a black man who in human form had hair like lamb's wool. The stories of "Africans who shaped our faith" also force us to learn the economic, social, and political history of the Bible—to focus on its context—as a method of better understanding and making relevant God's Word. See Appendix 1 for more information on Africans in the Bible.

Understanding the mission of the church of God. Though we may worship in predominantly African American congregations and live together in urban and suburban neighborhoods, Christ has called us to make disciples of all nations (Mark 16:15). While we must acknowledge and celebrate who we are, what we have survived and overcome, and where we are headed, our long-term vision must be centered on an awareness that God created the world and all people and things in it. As a result, our African-centeredness cannot be an excuse to elevate our culture above others; rather, it must focus on understanding who we are and our particular role in the building of God's kingdom on earth.

Music in Africentric Christian education. African American music is rich and moving, accompanying the spirit of our worship, serving as a backdrop for our prayers, and forming choral and congregational opportunities for praise through song. Christian education can teach the history, development, and traditions of the anthems, spirituals, gospel music, hymns (meter form and those in the Wesleyan tradition), and praise songs that accompany our worship.

Geography in Africentric Christian education. Maps are political tools. Most maps provide a view of Africa that is not accurate from a proportional perspective. In most maps, Africa, for example, appears much smaller than the landmass that was formerly called the Soviet Union, though measurements indicate that Africa is 11.6 million square miles and the Soviet area comprises 8.7 million square miles.[8] The maps most commonly used in educational venues are based on modernizations of the Mercator map, accurately designed in 1569 for navigational purposes.[9] However, to best understand the Bible and view the impact of Africa on biblical history, Peters Projection maps provide an accurate proportional view. African American Christian education elucidates the mysteries of the Bible when it re-educates church members through the accurate use of maps.

Designing programs that infuse rather than confuse. Some African American churches consider that African-centered Christian education is the use of black religious materials for Sunday school, celebration of Black History Month, and the occasional wearing of African clothing. Effective Africentric Christian education does more than this, however. It thoroughly infuses African-centered values and beliefs into all of its programs (worship, classes, and activities). If, for example, the preacher teaches from the pulpit that Jesus, in human form, was a man of dark-hued skin, providing biblical evidence and support for these statements, this lesson can serve as a model for other in-church teaching.

An African-Centered Philosophy of Christian Education

African-centeredness in Christian education focuses on the learning needs of the black Christian community. According to Dr. Okechukwu Ogbonnaya, the African-centered philosophy of Christian religious education actively creates and supports the development of a community with shared Christian values. "The church is being called on in the next millennia to equip the saints with various tools for being the church which will help transform community.... The church is being called to be an effective educational body for the ministry of Jesus Christ. Through its education, the church must give birth to people who are able to carry on intelligent discussions about their personal Christianity based on accurate information and evangelistic efforts dedicated to ministry inside and outside the local church."[10]

Concerned that most churches limit their capacity for Christian education by viewing it in a limited fashion (Sunday school only) and by focusing on the exclusive use of European teaching models, Dr. Ogbonnaya suggests several ways to use an African world view to develop effective Christian education methods. (See Table 3 on page 42.)

African American Approaches to Christian Education in Changing Times

Building on our history, new times require new responses. Departments of Christian education in the black church must address new attitudes and social realities and consider new approaches if our Christian education programs are to become more relevant, vital, and successful in their contributions to the ministry of the church. Observing that Christ spent his life among those undervalued by society, the ministries in African American churches provide for "the least, the last, and the lost" among us (and including us).

In addition to traditional home and foreign missions and monetary and other donations to the poor, ministries in our churches increasingly provide services to those with specific needs—homeless populations, persons infected with or affected by HIV/AIDS, incarcerated men, teen parents, married couples, and those who seek to understand

Table 3: African-Centered Strategies for Creating a Christian Community

Approaches[11]	Strategies[12]

Initiate members into the Christian community	• Create an atmosphere of support for persons involved in traditional Christian education classes and worship (use greeters, learn names of new persons, assign prayer partners).
	• Develop meaningful programs and rituals:
	  • African-centered infant dedication
	  • New members classes that meet congregation's needs
	  • Rites of Passage youth programs
	  • Special celebrations (rituals that celebrate the life of the church–anniversaries, ordinations–and the people of the church–births, graduations, marriages, and other accomplishments)

Get everyone involved	• The church is a community of believers. It must be a comfortable place to share personal and communal triumphs and sorrows.
	• Share personal and communal experiences through:
	  • Use of testimonies
	  • Use of Christian and church-specific rituals
	  • Training youth involvement in worship
	  • Active support of ministries designed to help those in need

Support equal teacher-student interaction	• The role of the teacher is to guide the class, not to act as the all-knowing expert. • Understand that students are teachers as well. Encourage students to contribute their knowledge and experiences to class discussions.
Encourage meaningful conversation	• Be discovery oriented. Each Christian education moment is an opportunity to create excitement about the love of Jesus through a communal discovery of new ways to interpret old truths. • Encourage spontaneity and creativity–there is no such thing as a wrong answer. Those in Christian education classes and experiences must feel that each question and perspective is valid, valued, and respected.
Apply critical thinking	• Name, explain, and analyze religious ideas. Don't just present them as fact. • Encourage the asking of questions, even those that express doubt. It is from questions that knowledge grows.
Reintegrate knowledge into the community	• Connect the context of Christian education to worship. For example, sermons can be based on the Bible verses or themes used in Sunday school or other classes. • Remember that Christian education occurs through every program, practice, and ritual of the local church. • Evangelize. Enlarge the definition of community by sharing the love of Jesus in the community outside of the church.

how to be better spouses, employees, friends, church members, and responsible men and women of God. These ministries are not separate from Christian education. In fact, anyone who entered a ministry-oriented church as a new member would immediately learn how that particular church viewed specific social issues, valued certain populations, and set expectations for the involvement of its membership in service to others.

TEACHABLE MOMENT

If history is important to the oppressor, it is a matter of life and death to the oppressed, who cannot find themselves or free themselves until they find and free their history.

Lerone Bennett, undated quotation

As we address theological correctness, social issues, and needs within the African American Christian community, Christian education requires that we ask and actively seek answers to essential questions that can enhance our understanding of who we are in Christ and what God is calling us to be to him and to one another.

- Does Christ—his life, his message, his sacrifice, and his saving grace—have special meaning for African Americans?
- What do the teachings of Christ contribute to our understanding of our struggles against injustice and inequality?
- As a group, how do we understand a God who permits suffering?
- How have we contributed to our own suffering? Does "**cultural backsliding**"[13] keep us from attaining the kingdom of God?
- Is there a word from the Lord meant just for us?

Notes

1. *Raphael Philemon Powell, "A Prayer for Freedom (1952)," in James Melvin Washington, Ph.D.* Conversations with God: Two Centuries of Prayers by African Americans. *New York: HarperCollins Publishers, 1994, page 195.*
2. *C. Eric Lincoln and Lawrence H. Mamiya.* The Black Church in the African

American Experience. *Durham, N.C.: Duke University Press, 1990, pages 52–53.*

3. *The issue of education has become controversial in some African American churches and communities. For example, not all churches continue to believe, as did the early AME church, that seminary training should be a requirement for ministers.*

4. *Dwight N. Hopkins.* Heart and Head: Black Theology—Past, Present and Future. *New York: Palgrave for St. Martin's Press, 2002, page 77.*

5. *Quoted by Dr. Forrest Harris.* Theology from a Black Baptist Perspective. *Seminar VI, Ministers' Division of the National Baptist Congress of Christian Education, St. Louis, Missouri, June 17–21, 2002, page 129.*

6. *Robert M Franklin.* Another Day's Journey: Black Churches Confronting the American Crisis. *Minneapolis, Minnesota: Fortress Press, 1997, page 43.*

7. *Dr. Jeremiah A. Wright, Jr. (A Study of 10 Biblical Personalities) and Colleen Birchett, Editor (Historical Overviews and Bible Study Applications).* Africans Who Shaped Our Faith. *Chicago: Urban Ministries, Inc. 1995, page 12.*

8. *www.google.com, keyword: Peters Projection Maps, accessed September 1, 2002.*

9. *Mercator had to make a map based on compass lines in order for it to be useful for navigational purposes, a process that lost the correct proportions of the continents. His purpose was to help sailors plot courses across oceans, and his map was well designed for that purpose.*

10. *A. Okechukwu Ogbonnaya, Ph.D.* African Ways: A Christian Education Philosophy. *Chicago: Urban Ministries, Inc., 2001, page 21.*

11. *Summarized from statements made by Dr. Ogbonnaya in* African Ways, *page 21.*

12. *Based on the recommendations of Dr. Ogbonnaya, these strategies and ideas are proposed by the author.*

13. *Coined by the author, the term **cultural backsliding** reflects our occasional adherence to a culture of victimization. While our history of oppression has put huge blocks in our way, we have sometimes created walls from those blocks rather than knocking them down. If Joshua could encircle his city with God's help, we, too, can make the walls of our Jericho tumble.*

Top Ten Tips for Enhancing or Establishing African-Centered Christian Education in the Local Church

1. Correct your theology—connect African American Christians to their actual Christian history.

2. View Christian education as a tool for liberation.

3. Consider Christian teaching to be a vocation and a craft.

4. See opportunities for Christian education in all classes, programs, and activities of the church.

5. Use Christian religious education to create and support a community of believers.

6. Assess the learning needs of your congregation.

7. Be honest about your teaching style, skills, and improvement needs.

8. Ask hard questions.

9. Encourage African American Christians to take personal responsibility for their circumstances.

10. Be prayerful about the tasks, goals, and expected outcomes of Christian education.

Preparation for the Journey

1. What do I contribute to the craft of Christian teaching in the African American church?

2. What changes must I make to enhance my skills as an African-centered Christian educator?

3. How do I support the learning needs of other Christian educators?

4. How does the Christian education program in my church focus on liberating the lives and thinking of its participants (students)?

5. How must I work with other Christian educators to create a supportive community of Christian believers?

6. How do I provide a framework that assists African American Christians in addressing issues of religious and cultural backsliding?

7. What strategies and resources might aid me in creating educational praxis?

8. What is my preparation for Christian teaching? (Consider issues of faith, experience, and training, and, importantly, an accurate and broad view of African and African American history.)

9. What experiences can I share with others that contribute to the growth of our African-centered Christian community?

10. What is the most important lesson I have learned from my Christian education students?

CHRISTIAN EDUCATION

Christian Education

Greg Ogden. *Discipleship Essentials: A Guide to Building Your Life in Christ.* Downers Grove, Illinois: Intervarsity Press, 1998. Designed to be used for individuals or small groups, this workbook walks readers through important questions about faith, encourages Bible study, provides a reading theme for each week, and asks questions that require thoughtful responses about the personal commitment of readers to live for Christ.

Patricia Beall Gruits. *Understanding God.* Rochester, Michigan: Peter Pat Publishers, 1985. This book presents questions and answers that address a broad range of issues about the God of the Old and New Testaments, our relationship to God, God's expectations of us, and the life, miracles, teachings, sacrifices, death, and resurrection of Jesus. It is a wonderful tool for new and established church members and a useful preparation tool for Christian educators.

Ward L. Kaiser and Denis Wood. *Seeing Through Maps: The Power of Images to Shape Our World View.* Amherst, Massachusetts: ODT, Inc., 2001. 800-736-1293 or www.google.com, keyword: Peters Projection Map. The Peters Projection Map provides an "area accurate map" for understanding the proportions of the world's landmasses. The map and books about the map's development and use can be purchased by phone or through the listed website.

Steven Tsoukalas. *Christian Faith 101: The Basics and Beyond.* Valley Forge: Judson Press, 2000. This user-friendly guidebook was written to teach new believers and laypersons the basics of Christian theology and, as such, is an excellent resource for Christian education teachers.

African-Centered Christian Education

James Abbington. *Let Mt. Zion Rejoice! Music in the African American Church*. Valley Forge: Judson Press, 2001. Sacred music is a way of praising God and serves as a wonderful ministry tool, teaching theology through hymns and rejoicing through praise songs. This book "provides practical and specific advice for choosing musical styles and repertoire based on your congregation's identity and worship goals." Dr. Abbington also suggests planning worship and music around a lectionary (a calendar and schedule that bases the content of services on events in the Christian year).

Holy Bible: African American Jubilee Edition. New York: American Bible Society, 1999. This version of the Bible is designed to "bridge the teachings of the Bible with the realities of African American day-to-day living." It includes accurate proportional mapping of the Holy Land.

Dwight N. Hopkins. *Head and Heart: Black Theology—Past, Present and Future*. New York: Palgrave for St. Martin's Press, 2002. This book discusses the history of black theology and the manner in which it applies to a post-affirmative action era.

Craig S. Keener and Glenn Usry. *Black Man's Religion: Can Christianity Be Afrocentric?* Downers Grove, Illinois: Intervarsity Press, 1996. Though African American Christians were subject to abuse at the hands of European Christians, these authors demonstrate that racism is not inherent in Christianity. In a painstakingly researched book, the authors demonstrate that "world history is also our history and the Bible is also our book."

Craig S. Keener and Glenn Usry. *Defending Black Faith: Answers to Tough Questions About African-American Christianity*. Downers Grove, Illinois: Intervarsity Press, 1997. This book debunks the incorrect perception that Christianity is the "white man's religion," addressing themselves to writers who challenge "African American Christianity itself" (rather than traditions of African American Christianity). Questions that are addressed include: Did the Christian gospels begin in Africa?, How do we answer the Nation of Islam?, and How do we answer orthodox Muslims?

C. Eric Lincoln and Lawrence H. Mamiya. *The Black Church in the African American Experience.* Durham: Duke University Press, 1990. By combining historical information, data from 1,800 interviews with urban and rural clergy, and an understanding of the impact of contemporary culture on the church, this book by respected scholars provides important information about the "most independent, stable, and dominant institution in black communities."

Olin P. Moyd. *The Sacred Art: Preaching and Theology in the African American Tradition.* Valley Forge: Judson Press, 1995. According to the author, preaching is teaching for which theology is the guiding light. "Theology," he says, "is like a mother guiding her child in the swimming pool to keep the child from going into the deep end.... Preaching's role in theology is similar to that of a father teaching his child how to drive a car in and through an urban downtown setting" (page 9).

A. Okechukwu Ogbonnaya, Ph.D. *African Ways: A Christian Education Philosophy.* Chicago: Urban Ministries, Inc., 2001. This book presents ideas about how to structure Christian religious education from an African world view. Its key theological assumption is that people of African descent learn through an approach that values community.

Cheryl Sanders, editor. *Living the Intersection: Womanism and Afrocentrism in Theology.* Minneapolis, Minnesota: Fortress Press, 1995. As influential cultural currents, womanism and Afrocentrism heighten our awareness of the importance of African American women in our religious beliefs and practice. "As womanism mines the ways and wisdom of African American women for Christian theology, so Afrocentricity excavates an African past to liberate the oppressed from Eurocentric world views."

James Melvin Washington, Ph.D., editor. *Conversations with God: Two Centuries of Prayers by African Americans.* New York: HarperCollins, 1994. This anthology of 235 years of African American prayers demonstrates the faith of our foreparents, teaches us the rudiments of prayer, and keeps us connected to our history.

Ann Streaty Wimberly. *Soul Stories: African American Christian Education.* Nashville: Abingdon Press, 1994. This practical tool for teaching Christian education to adults uses the African and African American oral tradition of storytelling as its primary strategy, with associated reflection exercises and activities.

Jeremiah A. Wright, Jr. (author) and **Colleen Birchett** (editor). *Africans Who Shaped Our Faith: A Study of 10 Biblical Personalities.* Chicago, Illinois: Urban Ministries, Inc., 1995. Rev. Wright discusses common misperceptions about Christianity as the "white man's religion," providing scriptural evidence that people in the Bible were Africans and questioning how they came to be represented as European Jews.

Other Christian Education Resources

Paulo Freire. *Pedagogy of the Oppressed.* New York: The Seabury Press, 1970. This classic text presents Freire's revolutionary ideas about education for oppressed people, focusing on techniques for creating informal educational opportunities that empower people through meaningful dialogues to which they contribute.

Lyle E. Schaller. *What Have We Learned? Lessons for the Church in the 21st Century.* Nashville: Abingdon Press, 2001. Designed to provide readers with some of the best thinking on congregational life, this book provides lessons on evangelism, multiculturalism, stewardship, worship, communication, and other topics to aid churches in meeting God's vision for them.

Norman Shawchuck and Roger Heuser. *Leading the Congregation: Caring for Yourself While Serving the People.* Nashville: Abingdon Press, 1993. Understanding that effective servants lead balanced lives, this book describes new models of church leadership.

Paul Taylor. *The Texts of Paulo Freire.* Buckingham: Open University Press, 1993. This text provides a simple way to read critique of the educational writings of Paulo Freire.

Dale Wiley. *Telling the Old, Old Story in Hymns.* Concerned about the decline of hymns and the theology that they teach through congregational ritual, Wiley has produced CDs that capture the traditions built by these time-tested songs. (They can be purchased through the websites of online booksellers. An audio interview with the author is available on NPR (March 29, 2002). Accessed on September 9, 2002, it can be found at www.npr.org/programs under "morning features, 2002."

Christian Education Websites

Denominational websites tend to include their own sections on Christian education strategies and materials, as well as links to other sites that Christian educators may find useful.

American Baptist Churches, **www.abc-usa.org**. The website has an Educational Ministries link that provides information about discipleship and stewardship, as well as educational materials (books and curricula) through Judson Press, its publishing house. (Accessed September 9, 2002.)

Barna Research Online, **www.barna.org**. This website provides statistics on religion and religious practice in the United States, offering comparisons between racial and ethnic groups. See "Archives, African Americans." (Accessed September 10, 2002.)

Stories Behind Hymns, **www.tanbible.com**. This site tells the stories that informed traditional Christian hymns. (Accessed September 9, 2002.)

United Church of Christ, **www.ucc.org**. This award-winning website explains the tenets of the faith, provides historical church information and documents, and has a detailed section on Christian education, including the church's educational mission, an education forum, and curriculum support. (Accessed September 9, 2002.)

United Methodist Churches, **www.umc.org**. This website provides a history of the church, links to UMC churches around the nation, an online magazine that profiles church programs and current issues, strategies for engaging in the Great Commission, and access to official church documents, including financial information that describes how ministry is conducted in the United States and around the world. (Accessed September 9, 2002.)

African American Christian Education Websites

These denominational and convention websites provide an array of information that can be used for educational purposes, specifically for teaching church members the history of their faith or facts about the groups with which their local church affiliates.

African Methodist Episcopal Zion Church, **www.theamezionchurch.org.** This site provides historical information about the faith that is useful for new members classes, as well as links to seminaries and to AME Zion churches around the country. (Accessed September 9, 2002.)

Black and Christian.com, **www.blackandchristian.com.** Dedicated to the provision of support to African American churches, this site provides clergy and leadership resources (The Pulpit); family ministry and African American website links (The Pew); theological resources for scholars, educators, and students (The Academy); historical and reference material on the African American church (The Black Church); and links to Africa and the diaspora (BNC Global). (Accessed September 9, 2002.)

Church of God In Christ, **www.cogic.org.** COGIC history, doctrine, and statements of faith are available online, as is access to the bookstore and educational videos. (Accessed September 9, 2002.)

National Baptist Convention USA, Inc., **www.nationalbaptist.com.** The website of the largest of the African American Baptist conventions provides information on the history of the organization and links to its Congress of Christian Education and to the American Baptist Churches website. (Accessed September 9, 2002.)

Progressive National Baptist Convention, **www.pnbc.org.** This website provides a wealth of information about the history of the organization that can be used to teach members of local churches affiliated with the convention. (Accessed September 9, 2002.)

BASIC TEACHING SKILLS AND LEARNING STRATEGIES

SEEING THE HAND OF GOD IN SCIENCE

Brain Behavior, Learning Styles, and Teaching Strategies

There is healing in your Word,
Deliverance in your Word,
Salvation in your Word,
Send your Word.
Your Word can save sinners,
Reclaim backsliders,
Encourage believers,
Send your Word.[1]

CHRISTIAN EDUCATORS ILLUMINATE THE WORD OF GOD THROUGH effective teaching. Effective teaching must use new strategies that take into account current information on brain behavior, learning styles, and the creation of optimal learning environments. Advances in science have allowed those involved in the study of learning to discover more about the human brain in the last half century than in the four previous centuries.[2] In recent years neurologists, psychiatrists, psychologists, master teachers, and learning specialists have used this knowledge to inform and change traditional teaching strategies and to enhance our understanding of how the brain learns.[3]

How the Brain Learns Best

Christian educators can become more effective in their teaching by understanding the ways that the brain works for most learners. Because all learning is based on the capacity of the brain to accept, process, and prioritize information, all teachers must possess a basic understanding of the manner in which the average brain senses, processes, remembers, and uses information. The learning brain is a marvelous gift from God.

Brains use many functioning pathways. The brain is exquisitely designed for processing lots of kinds of information. Simply put, one part of the brain processes spoken language and another responds to music. Yet other parts of the brain are responsive to emotions, color, visual stimuli, touch, taste, and graphic information like navigating city streets and map reading. Some parts of the brain work together to coordinate activities, like walking and talking, that use a variety of pathways at the same time. While the average brain has all of these neural pathways and organizational capabilities, these capacities are relatively weaker and stronger in different individuals.

- How can Christian educators demonstrate their understanding that brains function in different ways? Because learners have individual learning needs, Christian educators must use a number of teaching strategies to be respectful of the strengths and weaknesses of the brain, learning preferences, academic exposures, and communication styles of their students. (See "Teaching to Learning Styles," pages 57–60, and specific teaching strategies in the remainder of Section Two.)

Brains require active rest. Brains are active processing units. Though different in ways that this book cannot address, brains, like computers, are organisms that process, retrieve, discard, prioritize, and use information. Like computers, brains fatigue (in brains this is called "**neural fatigue**"). They process and recover over and over again—this is why deep sleep is important. It is the time in which tired brains recharge themselves by changing their brain wave patterns and temporarily altering the balance of their chemical compositions. Overloaded brains slow down and, if not properly refreshed, "lose" information (like computers, brains never actually lose information, though we may not be able to find the information that we are seeking).

- How can Christian educators demonstrate their understanding that brains need active rest? In an effort to get God's Word to the people (and because early service always ends late and cuts into Sunday school time, or the teacher has overprepared and wants to get every bit of information to her classes), Christian educators often present too much information at a time. Evening classes occur when adults have worked all day and have responsibilities to address when they get home—their bodies and their brains are tired. Christian educators frequently do not present information in a way that meets multiple learning needs or give learners adequate time to think about (process) information and put it into a meaningful personal context. Active rest can also be aided by giving restroom breaks at regular intervals.

Brains seek meaning. Information is a jumble from which our brains make meaning. Every time we open our eyes we see color, shape, and texture. Our brains make sense of this vast array of visual input—the brain's skill at seeking visual meaning helps us tell the difference between our best friend and a chair. Our ears bring to us language, music, and noise; our brains help us sort the new from the familiar. Touch teaches us what is hot or cold, soft or hard, comforting or painful. Repeated exposure to the same sets of stimuli creates memory—we recognize our mothers' voices as infants because they attend to our needs when we cry. Memory, in turn, connects to emotion. When our brain connects the smell of baking cookies with a hug from a loving grandmother, or when the scent of salt water on a sunny day recalls fishing trips with our fathers, we turn a complex series of visual, auditory, tactile, and emotional information into a meaningful and memorable moment.

- How can Christian educators demonstrate their understanding that brains seek meaning? Christian teachers should seek to make meaningful moments for those they teach. Teach in a way that appeals to the senses—primarily the eyes and ears—moving between them so as not to fatigue any one system. Use activity and participation to create opportunities for physical movement. Christian educators are also effective when they enhance the meaning of their teaching by connecting memory and experience to God's Word and facilitate opportunities for learners to learn actively through discussion and activity.

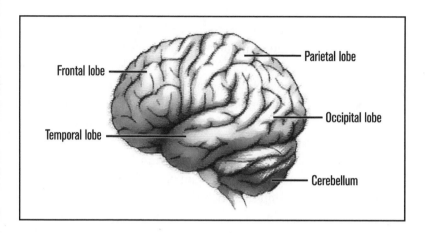

Parts of the Brain

The cerebral cortex, the computer-like portion of the brain, is the thin layer on the brain's surface that includes lobes or sections that control a variety of essential functions:[4]

Occipital lobe: processes vision and is located at the base of the head.

Temporal lobe: processes hearing, speech, and language.

Parietal lobe: processes sensory (touch) information.

Prefrontal lobe: allows us to plan and rehearse future actions. It is connected to the portion of the brain that processes and helps regulate emotions (the limbic system).

Frontal lobe: the area where critical thinking and problem solving occur.

Limbic system: controls emotions, related perceptions, and long-term memory.

Cerebellum: controls balance and automatic movements.

Teaching to learning styles addresses the functions of the brain and meets the complex informational needs of most learners.

Teaching to Learning Styles

In every venue in which Christian education is provided, Christian educators will need to address several basic learning styles: auditory (related to hearing), visual (related to sight), kinesthetic or sensory (related to touch), and relational (a form of learning necessary for the creation of the Christian community and an important form of learning for most African Americans). While most persons rely on one learning style and can identify it as their strength by the time they are young adults, others are multimodal learners who respond well to materials that address several of their senses. While there is some research that indicates that African American learners tend towards auditory and relational learning styles, the truth is that African Americans learn through many senses, the same senses as all other racial and ethnic groups. For example, as the primary venue in which Christian education occurs, worship in the African American church is a perfect mixture of experiences and information that address all learning styles. We touch and agree (**tactile** and relational), clap our hands and become Spirit-filled (kinesthetic), listen to sermons and songs (auditory and relational), and pay close attention to the sights we experience as we recognize friends (visual and relational), notice that the hat Ms. Sara is wearing has blocked our view of the guest preacher (visual and relational), and avoid Deacon Jones because we have not honored our tithe as we promised God and him (relational). See Section Three, "Succeeding in a Variety of Christian Education Venues and Formats," for more information on Christian education venues.

Characteristics of Auditory Learners

Auditory learners are most adept at learning from what they hear and tend to have strong memories for information presented to them in oral form. They tend to respond best to traditional lecture-format teaching styles. Characteristics of auditory learners typically include:

- The capacity to retain information discussed in groups or heard in conversations and lectures
- Effective verbal communication skills with which they can clearly articulate beliefs and views
- A love of language, large vocabularies, and attention to the accurate use of words
- Enjoyment of discussions
- The tendency to talk through challenging concepts
- Discomfort with silence

- The likelihood of being easily distracted by sound
- Ease of learning foreign languages
- Good writing skills
- Musical ability

Strategies for teaching auditory learners include:
- Lectures
- Group discussions
- Asking them to summarize the major themes addressed in a class, workshop, or seminar
- Using a variety of auditory methods—discussion, lecture, song, and class readings
- Varying the tone and pitch of your voice and the emphasis placed on words to maintain learner interest

Characteristics of Visual Learners
Visual learners are excellent processors of what they see. They benefit from visual presentations such as PowerPoint and from charts, diagrams, pictures, written instructions, and course materials. They are likely to take notes in classes to aid in their memory and retention of learned information. Characteristics of visual learners often include:
- Good descriptive abilities
- Attention to visual details
- Remembering what is seen and read
- Ability to manipulate visual information
- Reliance on written materials, to-do lists, class notes, and appointment calendars as learning aids and memory cues
- Better recall of faces than names
- Difficulty retaining information presented in a traditional lecture format

Teaching strategies for visual learners include:
- Providing handouts that outline class contents or that list important points
- Illustrating lecture points with visual aids (PowerPoint, overhead projectors, laser pointers, maps, artwork)

- Art activities
- Allowing time for learners to check notes and other written references in response to questions or as a way to organize their thoughts
- Computer-based projects
- Use of timelines as memory aids for historical events
- Teaching materials that include photographs, charts, and graphs in addition to written information
- Varying the types of visual information to maintain interest

Characteristics of Kinesthetic Learners

Kinesthetic learners learn by doing. Retention of information is aided by movement, touch, and the experience of materials used in learning activities. While this is often a learning style associated with young children, many adults are also kinesthetic learners. Most successful and engaged when actively participating in a learning activity, kinesthetic learners benefit from hands-on teaching techniques. Characteristics of kinesthetic learners usually include:

- Learning by activating large and small muscle groups
- A need to touch materials used in projects
- Note taking (adults)
- Interacting with people and objects to learn
- Physical demonstrativeness (touching, hugging, kissing)
- Difficulty sitting for extended periods
- Athletic prowess resulting from good physical control and timing

Teaching strategies for kinesthetic learners include:

- Computer-based projects
- Dramatic arts
- Liturgical dance
- Building projects
- Stand and stretch time and restroom breaks—though this may seem to be an unusual teaching strategy, kinesthetic learners signal teachers that their brains and bodies require recharging. They will learn more effectively if rest breaks are built into their schedules.
- Providing feedback made on projects
- Allowing adequate time for project completion

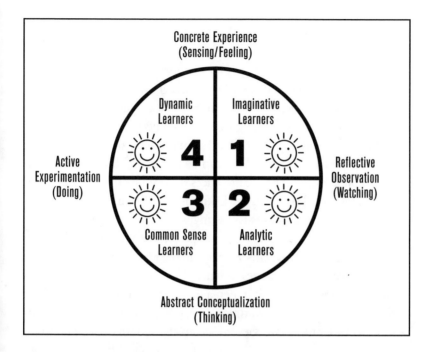

Other Learning Models

Although there are many learning models, more than can be easily discussed in this volume, they tend to have similarities to the model for auditory, visual, and kinesthetic learners that is presented here. As with other models, Christian education teachers will best meet the learning needs of their students if they present materials in a manner that addresses all learning styles described for a particular model. Another learning model, the 4MAT System by Bernice McCarthy, describes the following learning categories:

Imaginative Learners, in quadrant one, favor learning through sensing, feeling, and watching (visual and relational learning styles).

Analytic Learners, in quadrant two, favor learning by thinking and watching (visual and auditory learning styles).

Common Sense Learners, in quadrant three, prefer to learn by thinking and doing (kinesthetic style).

Dynamic Learners, in quadrant four, typically learn by sensing/feeling and doing (kinesthetic and relational styles).

Considerations for African American Learning Styles

Ella Pearson Mitchell tells us, "(Our history) is our well, and we need to quit thinking that black equals ignorant. It's high time our children know that God gave us these great signs of genius when Northern Europeans were just beginning to form as a people."

Though the brains of all of God's children are designed with the same capacity for learning, there can be cultural differences in learning style preferences. These differences are frequently a reflection of cultural practices. For example, Eskimos who live in snowy climates develop expert visual senses to distinguish animal tracks and traveling paths in what, to most, would appear to be an unending snowy landscape. Native Americans who live in the Plains (the Midwest) are noted to have excellent senses of smell that allow them to locate animals for hunting or to know when a territory has been invaded. West Africans, with a historical tradition of passing oral histories from generation to generation, are viewed as strong auditory learners. In all cases, cultural practice has caused these groups to attend more strongly to a particular sense though, it is important to note, they have access to all learning modes.

Educational specialist Janice Hale specializes in the learning needs of African Americans with particular attention to techniques for effectively teaching young black children, specifically those in educational systems that undervalue them as capable learners. Dr. Hale reports from years of research that we tend to learn best when the materials are culturally appropriate based on our history and experiences. The African American teaching strategies she recommends indicate that our learning styles are often:

Kinesthetic: many African Americans learn through activity

Affective: we tend to be relational and focused on the ways that we interact with one another (relational learning)

Oral: as descendents of those who passed wisdom and history through stories and music, we are comfortable with learning by hearing (auditory learning)

Dynamic: learners respond to exciting, interesting, creative, and well-presented materials, as these methods facilitate long-term memory.[5]

Teaching Relational Learners

Relational learners learn most effectively when they have developed strong and trusting relationships with their instructors. African Americans, as a group, are relational people. We tend to enjoy interactions with other people and use information obtained by body language to judge personality and character. As an example, the call and response component of African American worship reflects the intentional building of a relationship between parishioners and pastor. Our tendencies to make verbal responses to characters in movies and on television, and our verbal and physical encouragement (clapping, standing to acknowledge accomplishment) of those who participate meaningfully in church activities are additional evidence of our relational learning style. Raising holy hands represents the active recognition of a relationship that reveres and honors Christ.

TEACHABLE MOMENT

Relational Values

Despite living in a culture that is contrary to African values, we attempt to declare no division between the sacred and the secular in African American Christian churches. African-centeredness and African values flow through everything that we do…. Our [practice of] religion is relational—there is no separation between belief and action, between the head and the heart. We understand that the liturgy of praise and worship allows us to praise God and reap the blessings of relationships with him and his people.

Dr. Iva Carruthers, President, Urban Outreach Foundation, Chicago, Illinois, telephone interview, August 15, 2002

Characteristics of relational learners
- Attention to the body language of others
- Maintenance of eye contact
- Tendencies to create appropriate intimacy through touch (high fives)

- Creating distance through body language when relationships sour (ignoring, "talk to the hand" signals)[6]
- Finding opportunities for discussions
- Asking personal questions
- Sharing personal information

Communication strategies that are useful for relational learners include the use of the following behaviors in conjunction with the instructional methods recommended for auditory, visual, and kinesthetic learners:

- Smile
- Maintain eye contact
- Use touch when appropriate
- Relate stories and experiences related to the class, seminar, or workshop topic
- Be aware of your physical presence. Slouching, squinting, or apparent boredom distracts learners and communicates to them a lack of teacher interest in them and the subject matter.

Relationship Building Techniques

Know class members. Though class, seminar, and workshop membership may change from week to week, Christian educators should work to remember the names and circumstances of learners. People feel valued when they are remembered. Knowing class members also makes their contributions more meaningful to you and for other Christian education participants.

Create community. In seminars and workshops, make time for learners to introduce themselves to the group and talk briefly about their work, the length of their membership in the church, the ministries in which they are involved, and the reasons that they are involved in a specific class. Understanding "where people are coming from" allows teachers to anticipate interests and responses.

Use technology. Churches comfortable with the use of technology can have online class registration that provides Christian educators with information about their students ahead of time. Knowing in advance the interests of students can aid in teacher preparation of materials and questions likely to intrigue and engage them.

Basic Teaching Strategies

While specific strategies for working with learners of different ages and with different sets of learning needs will be addressed in other chapters of this section, Christian educators can greatly improve their teaching by using a number of basic strategies.

Questions that Encourage Discussion

Asking meaningful questions at the right time and in the right way is one of the most valuable tools of teachers. Educators must remember that in any classroom they will encounter brains with learning style preferences, brains that are at different points in their processes of active rest, and brains that need time to process information and retrieve data meaningful to the question that has been asked. In many cases, all of these activities will be happening at the same time in the same person. Using this knowledge, effective Christian educators will:

Ask one question at a time. Christian educators desire learners to focus on understanding specific concepts. This is aided by asking one question at a time and allowing time for learners to reflect on it and to retrieve information useful for addressing it. When Christian educators ask complex questions with many parts, different learners will hear and respond to different parts of the question, creating a disjointed discussion and a confusing learning experience.

Ask class, workshop, or seminar participants to generate questions. Active participation in using information presented in class to generate questions creates meaning for learners.

Wait for the class's response. Many teachers are tempted to supply answers themselves. However, the focus of Christian education is helping believers understand and apply Christian facts, principles, and expectations to their lives. They will have more meaningful learning experiences when they arrive at the answers themselves.

Acknowledge the learners' responses. All learners want to know that they have been heard. Asking other class members to comment on statements that have been made, acknowledgment of an interesting point or idea, and friendly body language send the message that responses are valued and respected.

Place responses in the context of the lesson. Effective teachers paraphrase the learner's response and place it within the context of the lesson, experience, or activity. This strategy helps all learners identify from that response principles that have meaning for them.

Ask a variety of questions. Effective questions will range from those that ask for the simple recall of facts to those that encourage students to apply Christian principles to their lives.

- Simple recall. These questions ask learners to remember basic facts held in their memories.
  - ○ *Sample questions based on simple recall:* Who wrote the Acts of the Apostles? To whom were the books of 1 and 2 Corinthians addressed?
- Comparison and contrast. These questions ask learners to figure out the similarities between and differences among facts and to place them in historical and social contexts.
  - ○ *Sample questions based on comparison and contrast:* What was unusual about the helpful attitude of the Good Samaritan to the man on the side of the road? What was the motivation of the writer of this book to address this issue (Luke 10:25-37)? How are our historical experiences as African American slaves similar to those of the ancient Egyptians? Suppose you were Puah, the midwife, and had to decide whether to obey orders to kill male Hebrew children at their birth (Exodus 1:15-21)? What would you choose to do? Why would you make that choice? What influenced Puah's decision? What factors might influence your decisions?
- Correlation. These questions ask learners to connect the dots, formulating creative and thoughtful ideas and hypotheses from a number of informational sources.
  - ○ *Sample questions based on correlation:* Our Sunday school lesson states that God's wisdom is more valuable than gold, silver, or rubies. What is the evidence for this? What passages of Scripture teach about the things that God values?
- Creative life application. Learners are asked to apply the principles from what they have learned to their lives, a process that contributes to the enhancement of meaning and memory.

○ *Sample questions based on creative life application:* If you were a man who had few resources, what would keep you from behaving like Judas? In what circumstances have you doubted God's presence in your life? What moved you from doubt to belief?

Use of Interesting Teaching Tools

Old modes of Christian education frequently keep us mired in the use of traditional materials such as Sunday school lessons or a strict reliance on reading passages of Scripture. Effective teaching requires use of a variety of interesting techniques and presentation of materials in a manner that captures learners' interest.

Vary materials. To keep learners interested, vary the materials that are used to teach. Daily newspapers provide a whole range of current events that can be used to generate discussions and to which Christian principles or interpretations can be applied.

Go to the movies. Use short videos or films that address points important in the life of Christians (child rearing techniques, meaningful and mutually respectful marital relationships, or difficult problems in families or with coworkers). Facilitate discussions based on film events. Have a set of prepared questions that address major issues. Ask students to generate questions or ask for a volunteer discussion leader.

Search for God in unusual places. A technique I frequently use with teenagers and adult learners is to ask everyone to bring a favorite magazine and look in it for evidence of God's truths. The responses will be interesting and inventive, creating opportunities for meaningful discussions. Congregations with computer learning centers can give assignments that ask learners to research religious issues online or to discuss the experience of using online prayer rooms and religious chat sites.

Bring the house down. Each community has African American theater events for which church groups often receive substantial discounts. Discussions about the plays provide unique ways for interpreting art through a Christian filter. Churches can also develop their own productions as ways to bring healing.

Walk with God. Another technique that classes often enjoy is to bring old photos of themselves to class, using them to discuss where they were on their Christian journey at the time that the photo was taken.

Interesting follow-up questions to this discussion are What would a picture taken today illustrate about your walk with God? Where would you be? What would you be doing? and Why?

Interview church leaders. To get more information on topics relevant to becoming a good Christian—the requirements for stewardship, **tenets** of one's faith, importance of tithing, the need to become involved in church ministries—African American Christian educators can ask their pastors, deacons, elders, and ministry leaders to make class presentations or sit for interviews by class participants.

Honor the living memories of senior saints. The history of a local church often resides in the memories of its senior saints. Invite older members to talk about the church and how it has changed over time.

TEACHABLE MOMENT

Maafa: The Healing Ship
St. Paul's Community Church, Brooklyn, New York

An African American pastor from Brooklyn, Reverend Johnny Ray Youngblood, says that healing the racial divide in America begins with his own people healing themselves. He believes that the legacy of slavery is at the root of black self-loathing and despair, and that "the only way out is back through" the trauma. Through a re-enactment of the African American experience of slavery, Reverend Johnny Ray Youngblood wants to move forward. It's called *Maafa,* Ki-Swahili for the "disaster" or "unimaginable horror" of slavery…. Reverend Youngblood says that the victims of any kind of trauma cannot heal until they fully acknowledge what they've been through. He says healthy survival means that the victims of any kind of trauma, even one like Columbine or the Federal Building bombing, must go through some sort of debriefing in order to move on. With the *Maafa,* he hopes to heal what he sees as a national wound that affects the African American population and the entire country, through a dramatic purging of the past.

Transcript, Osgood File, CBS Radio Network 8/10/01.
www.acfnewsource.org, accessed September 10, 2002

Traditional Materials Used in New Ways

The Bible is a major teaching tool for Christian educators. Encourage learners to bring different versions of the Bible (including the African American Jubilee Edition) so that passages can be examined from a number of perspectives. Use the references provided in each version to share information that enriches the discussion. Research (www.bibles.net; www.studylight.org) and discuss the reasons that each interpretation was developed.

Notes

1. *"Is There A Word From the Lord?" Copyright 1998, Glenn Burleigh, Burleigh Inspirations Music, www.glenmusik.com, P.O. Box 16091, Oklahoma City, Oklahoma, 73113, 405-232-7477. Used with permission.*

2. *Dr. Bruce D. Perry. "How the Brain Learns Best." www.google.com (keywords: how the brain learns best), accessed September 10, 2002.*

3. *Despite years of research that attempt to prove that persons of African origin have inferior brains, African American brains and brain functions are no different than those of other racial groups or cultures.*

4. *Copyright permission granted for educational uses by website message, www.nncc.org, accessed September 10, 2002.*

5. *Janice Hale and V. P. Franklin.* Learning While Black: Creating Educational Excellence for African American Children. *Baltimore: Johns Hopkins University Press, 2001, page 148.*

6. *Though this is decidedly un-Christian behavior, it describes the reaction of relational learners to difficult or confusing social interactions.*

CHAPTER SIX

JESUS LOVES
THE LITTLE CHILDREN

Effective Teaching and Learning for
Preschool and Elementary School Students

And every breath and heartbeat
Echoes praise to my village god;
I am a valued African gift
Made so by village love.[1]

THE JOY OF AFRICAN-CENTERED CHRISTIAN EDUCATION FOR CHILDREN is that it provides an opportunity to teach them about the love of Christ at the earliest points in their development. In the lives of young children, Christian education sows powerful seeds that establish values, teach beliefs, and develop a framework for living that helps them create strong personal relationships with Christ. For our children this training is also an important moment for teaching them African-centered theology, beliefs that are historically accurate, theologically sound, and scripturally verifiable. The teaching of African-centered Christian beliefs to young children allows Christian educators to help parents meet the requirement to "train a child in the way he should go, and when he is old he will not turn from it" (Proverbs 22:6).

Part of that teaching is required to correct terrible media messages that indicate that African Americans are, at worst, criminals or, at best, are relegated to roles as entertainers and athletes. While some of our children will be gifted as entertainers and athletes, they will find few public media models that encourage them to develop their minds. That is the role of public schools, which have too often failed our children, and of our churches, which have an opportunity to correct misperceptions about African American history.[2]

Adults involved in the lives of children as parents and teachers are responsible for training them. African American parents and Christian educators provide young children with essential tools, among which are feedback about desirable and unacceptable behaviors, information about social rules and expectations, a knowledge of the potential impact of racism on their lives and ways for them to succeed in spite of it, and learning experiences that help them develop the social, emotional, intellectual, and physical skills that, over time, allow them to lead independent, productive, and spirit-filled lives. It is especially important that this training happens early in life. Research indicates that appropriate parental love and attention are crucial for giving children the emotional security for learning from and interacting with others.

During early childhood, children learn how to operate in the world. They develop increasing mastery over their bodies, learning to walk, feed themselves, and take care of personal needs. They learn how to effectively communicate their needs to adults and how to form friendships with their peers. By the age of three, children have learned whom to trust and basic rules about right and wrong, the benefits of sharing, and the importance of being truthful.

At all ages, Christian educators must address learners at the appropriate developmental level. Christian education builds on skills developed in the home and practiced in preschool, kindergarten, and the early elementary grades. With minds not yet capable of complex reasoning, preschool and school-aged children need to focus on the basic facts of African-centered Christian education:

- Who is Jesus and why does he love us?
- How can we tell that we are made in the image of God?
- What is the Holy Book that God provided for us?
- What are some important events in the life of Jesus?
- Why do we celebrate Christmas?
- What is the importance of Easter?

Early childhood Christian education is also important for helping our children learn:

- Behaviors expected of Christians
- Church decorum
- Grace for meal times

- Prayers
- Bible verses
- Denominational tenets
- Names and roles of local church leadership
- Order of worship
- Church traditions and celebrations (holy days, church anniversaries, church picnics, and Vacation Bible School)

Goals of African-centered Christian Education for Preschool and School-aged Children

The primary goals of African-centered Christian education for young and school-aged children are to:
- Teach them about the love of Jesus
- Teach them Christian beliefs and practices
- Get them excited about living for Christ
- Help them identify ways to actively participate in the life of the church
- Create a new generation of youth trained in the traditions of the church
- Provide a safe and supportive haven where they learn self-love, personal discipline, and responsibilities to family and community
- Support future church leadership

Skills that Expert Christian Educators of Preschool and School-aged Children Bring to Their Classes

Christian educators of preschool and young school-aged children must:
- Share a joyful spirit
- Love learning as much as teaching
- Uncover the talents of each young student
- Put Christian learning in context
- Be passionate about teaching
- Build positive relationships with parents
- Demonstrate Africentric Christian values through behavior
- Motivate students to explore what they have learned outside of the classroom, placing it in a Christian context

TEACHABLE MOMENT

Faith Mountain: An Extreme Adventure with Jesus
Metropolitan Baptist Church, Washington, D.C.

Designed for Vacation Bible School students between the ages of two and twelve, Faith Mountain, a paper maché creation, stands as a large and tangible object in an auditorium. It is part of a plan to connect children to their faith through a series of age appropriate activities that present lessons based on Bible stories about men and women who pushed their faith to its limits. Considered one of the most important evangelistic efforts of the church, Vacation Bible School includes outreach to children who do not regularly attend church services. Children from two to five are on an adventure called "From the Pit to the Palace." Focused on the story of how Joseph proved his innocence and ascended to the throne, it teaches that God rewards personal faith. Six- to eight-year-olds engaged in "Face Your Giants" learn that God empowers the faithful with calls to ministry. "Destination Unknown" is the story of Abraham, Sarah, and Isaac shared with nine- and ten-year-olds to teach that the faithful trust and obey God even when they don't understand his demands. Samson has "The Ultimate Bad Hair Day," and involved eleven- and twelve-year-olds explore the truth that God forgives and restores to his fold those who repent. Interesting topics, age appropriate activities that are fun, and theology in game form simultaneously create memories and teach theology.

Faith Mountain is a purchased program (Standard Publishing ©2002) that MBC adapted for their population of children. See Chapter Eleven for information on adapting purchased materials.

Principles of Early Child Development and Learning for Preschoolers (Ages 2–5)

Early childhood learning is connected to developmental patterns of brain development, environmental enrichment provided in the home, hands-on experiences, personal relationships with other children and trusted adults, and an inborn curiosity about the world. These are the years of tremendous brain growth and development—children make connections because their brains are actively hard-wiring what they learn from the activities in which they are engaged. Exposure to interesting ideas, events, and people creates more complex connections and skills, while limited exposures lead to underdeveloped neural connections. Basic principles about child development indicate that children learn best when they:

Are physically and psychologically safe and secure. Learning environments should be warm, friendly, and accepting of each child. Christian educators should present to children the love of Jesus using smiles, appropriate touch, and a sense of fun.

Are active and creative. Sunday school, Vacation Bible School, and other Christian education classes for children between the ages of two and six must include play. Young children learn best through activities that allow them to experiment with, manipulate, and experience their environments. Play provides children with opportunities to use their imaginations and to place learned information in a social context. Actively involved in their fantasy lives, young children enjoy activities where they get to "make believe."

Have positive social interactions. Young children are learning to function independently. They will test their theories about the world, discovering if they are correct or incorrect as a result of feedback that they receive from other children and adults. Christian educators should provide learning environments that allow young children lots of opportunities to learn from one another through guided discussions, group activities, and positive comments.

Ask questions. Children need to make sense of their experiences; they learn by asking where, when, why, how, and who. Understandably, at a young age their experiences and ability to reason are somewhat limited. Parents, teachers, and Christian educators must be willing to answer their constant questions in a way that challenges their curiosity and motivates them to explore new ideas.

Are acknowledged as individuals. Despite their developmental similarities, children are remarkably different. They will learn best when Christian educators recognize the skills, talents, interests, and contributions made by each child. Such individualized attention actually strengthens the functioning of the learning group, models acceptance for the children, and makes each child feel valued and important.

Sing to the Lord. Children love music. It stimulates brain activity, encourages the use of memory skills, and is a fun and easy way to teach them Christian beliefs ("Jesus Loves the Little Children"), components of worship ("Gloria Patri," "The Lord's Prayer," and praise songs), and songs important to the life of the African American church.

Feel loved. God is love, and children must feel loved in his church. Because the world can be a disaffirming place for many African American children, the church must affirm their strengths, work with their families to teach them pride in themselves as individuals and in their role as Christians, and in the rich traditions of their racial and faith heritages.

Principles of Early Child Development and Learning for Elementary School Students (Ages 6–11)

As is necessary with younger children, those who teach school-aged children must be aware of their typical learning styles and their developmental needs. Their attention spans are expanding, they are interested in real events and people (birthday parties, sports, grandma's visit, real and imagined distressing personal interactions), they have specific interests and skills, are increasingly social, and are focused on learning and following rules.

Elementary School Children Ages 6–8

Though they are actively involved in learning and are capable of processing information in more complicated ways, brain growth and development have reached a temporary plateau in six- to eight-year-old children. Young school-aged children are focused on building basic academic skills, exploring personal interests, and learning social rules and behavioral expectations. This age group learns best when they:

Work in teams. Young school-aged children are learning the processes involved in successful teamwork such as being a good sport, winning and losing gracefully, sharing team resources, and performing to the best of one's ability. In these processes they apply and internalize prior learning. Christian education for this age group should provide lots of small group activities where children can work on class projects, play Christian learning games, and help each other with class activities.

Practice writing skills. Writing skills are new, and children love the opportunity to practice them. Age-appropriate Christian education materials should include Bible stories that they can color and describe in short sentences that they write or copy.

Copy. Copying materials is a way of encoding them. Children enjoy copying because it gives them mastery over fine motor (hand-eye coordination) skills and provides them with a finished product in a short amount of time. Children will enjoy Christian education materials that allow them to copy short Bible verses or complete fill-in-the-blanks.

Engage in organized play. Games have rules, and rules teach expectations for conduct. Children love games because they get to practice and remember rules, demonstrate skills in a board game or a sport, and enjoy the company of friends. Christian games are available from Christian bookstores and online resources such as those found at www.kidssundayschool.com.

Get positive feedback for their efforts. Children are developing skills of which they are proud but gain confidence in themselves only when we praise them for a job well done. Praise should be presented in whole sentences that describe the reason for a compliment that is given. "What a lovely picture of Jesus" or "I was so proud of how you held your head up high when you recited your part in the Easter pageant" are more effective forms of praise than "Good job, Johnny." At this age Johnny is doing so much so quickly that he may not know what he has done that is deserving of praise.

Elementary School Children Ages 9–11

Children between the ages of nine and eleven are increasingly confident about their basic academic skills and have defined personalities as well as strongly stated likes and dislikes. They are concerned with gaining social acceptance, developing same sex friendships (this is the age of "best friends"), and cementing those friendships through the development of elaborate rituals ("blood brothers," passwords for entry into special membership clubs, fancy handshakes, dance steps, and made-up words or specialized ethnic, regional, or other imaginative uses of language). Additionally, children of this age are beginning to pay attention to social pressures from peers to conform to standards that may not match those of their parents or the church. This age group learns best when they are:

Affirmed. While many of the goals of the civil rights era have been attained, there remain far too many instances that remind us that many people hold African American children to low standards, not expecting them to achieve or succeed in their efforts. African American Christian educators must affirm for their young students their high expectations for excellence in all realms, while providing the support, encouragement, and information that facilitates success in activities and pride in self.

Engaged in dramatic projects. Children in this age group love to work in groups and to plan events. Dramatic projects give them the opportunity to use their developing skills in real life situations that recreate Bible stories and are presented to an admiring and supportive church family.

Involved in guided discussions. As evidence of the strength of active childhood learning, I still recall Sunday school classes in which we recreated Bible stories (Daniel in the lion's den, the Christians and the lions, David and Goliath, Jonah in the belly of the whale, Moses freeing his people), and discussed how we felt in each situation. These discussions, facilitated by teachers, helped us understand the human responses described in the Bible stories, allowed us to apply the principles of those stories to our young lives and, importantly, stayed in our memories as reflections of Christian history and beliefs, and as evidence of God's presence in our lives.

Involved in small groups. Though at this age teamwork sometimes becomes competitive, 9- to 11-year-old school-aged children learn well in groups. They are able to test their theories about life in discussions with their church friends. Because children at this age can sometimes become too competitive, Christian educators must set clear behavioral expectations.

Monitored from afar. Though close adult supervision annoys this age group (they are quick to let adults know that they are not babies and can do things on their own), they are not emotionally prepared to be truly independent. Christian educators should provide them with activities, talk about rules for behavior and expectations for task completion, then check in with them from time to time, walking around the room to see the progress of each small group.

Allowed to participate in worship. Worship service is where a lot of basic Christian education comes together for children of this age. Having been taught the Lord's Prayer, they now recite it with the entire congregation. Having learned about the order of worship, they are comforted by the routine pattern of the service—children of this age love predictability. They are also old enough to have roles in adult worship on occasion. They can be trained by Christian educators to read Scripture, greet visitors, provide creative arts and activities that are meaningful in the worship context, and make special announcements in church. Churches that provide special worship services for children allow them to regularly practice these skills and to participate in worship that is better timed for their attention spans.

Encouraged to share their experiences. As is the case with all children of this age, African American children are bombarded with images from the media and from other children that influence their behavior. African American children have an additional burden, however, in that many of the media messages they receive are directed against traditional black values that focus on self-pride and self-control, familial expectations for good behavior, academic excellence, respect for elders, and contributions to the larger community. To guard against these negative messages or the negative influences found in some homes, the Christian educator can serve an essential community-building role simply by encouraging discussion that allows children to share their experiences and, with their peers, learn to use constructive problem-solving strategies.

Put on center stage. Children of this age are typically natural performers. They love singing in choirs and learn greatly from the discipline required to learn songs, march into the choir stand, and behave in a grownup manner in service, and they provide a ministry that is such an important part of worship. According to Dr. James Abbington, children's choir directors should be mindful that young children have limitations to vocal capabilities and should pick songs that are appropriate for immature voices.[3] Children also love liturgical dance, a process that allows them to be physically active while illustrating religious stories and songs through movement.

Designing Developmentally Appropriate Christian Education for Young and Elementary Children

To design programs appropriate for young children and those in elementary school, it is important to understand that, as they grow, children develop specific sets of skills. Their large and small motor abilities, social and emotional development, and cognitive capacities will determine the range of Christian education activities that they can successfully learn from and participate in.

Christian educators, particularly those working with mixed age groups, should be acquainted with the developmental expectations appropriate to children of different ages. The following tables provide developmental stage descriptions and activities for children ages two to four, five to seven, eight to nine, and ten to eleven. While the developmental descriptions and suggested activities are far from exhaustive, they are designed to illustrate child skills within various ages and to provide for Christian educators information that can be applied to Sunday school, Vacation Bible School, or other child-oriented church activities.

Physical Development
Physical development involves the strengthening of two sets of motor skills. Fine motor skills develop from our ability to make our hands do what we want them to. Reaching, grasping, handling scissors and eating utensils, using a remote control, brushing our teeth, dialing phone numbers, and using computers all involve hand-eye coordination, specifically the ability to control the movements of our fingers so that we can have an interaction with an object that we wish to use.

Gross motor development involves the controlled use of large muscle groups. Walking, running, climbing, sitting and standing, reaching, and clapping are all examples of gross motor activities.

Social Development
As they grow, children move from a total focus on their own needs to excitement about participating in groups and developing special friendships. Three-year-olds, for example, engage in parallel play—

Table 4: Physical Domain[4]

	Ages 2–4	Ages 5–7	Ages 8–9	Ages 10–11
Large Muscle Skills	• Walking • Running • Throwing • Catching • Clapping	• Running • Jumping • Throwing • Catching • Clapping	• Still gaining control over large muscles	• Good control of large muscles
Small Muscle Skills	• Tearing • Pasting • Drawing	• Cutting • Pasting • Drawing	• Good tool use	• Excellent tool use
Related CE Activities	• Color pictures of Christian themes • Learn simple Christian songs • Play simple games based on Christian themes	• Color pictures of Christian themes • Draw original pictures based on Christian themes • Play games based on Christian themes • Sing in children's choir	• Create original art based on biblical themes • Play games based on Christian themes • Children's choir • Africentric map making and reading	• Create original art based on biblical themes • Develop art projects that support church activities and programs • Children's choir and ushers • Africentric map making and reading

they stand next to each other while they play and are aware of the other's presence but are independently involved with their own learning and mastery of skills. Ten-year-olds, on the other hand, love activities that involve their group of best friends.

Emotional Development

For all age groups, self-esteem is aided by the achieving of success at academic tasks and in social relationships. Emotional development is aided by helping learners focus more on processes rather than outcomes and by giving them lots of positive feedback for their good efforts.

Table 5: Social Domain[4]

	Ages 2–4	Ages 5–7	Ages 8–9	Ages 10–11
Outside World	• Oriented to family • View adults as parental figures • Learning to share	• Oriented to family • View adults as parental figures	• Interested in communities • Interested in adult roles and job functions	• Interested in other cultures and customs
Related CE Activities	• Dress up • Work in groups of two or three • Learn simple Christian songs	• Family-centered roleplay • Work in groups of five or six • Sing Christian songs • Learn Bible verses • Color maps of the Holy Land	• Team activities and Christian games • Role play (structured by teacher) based on Bible stories • Map activities about the Holy Land • Make and send cards to children at partner churches	• Raise funds for missions and ministries • Discuss current events • Learn about different religious traditions • Roleplay (structured by students) based on Bible stories and current events • Volunteer in the community surrounding the church

Cognitive Development

The growth of a child's brain occurs rapidly through age three, then slows until the teen years. Mastery of skills is the main cognitive task for children in early and middle childhood. Children love routines that help them learn patterns and allow them to plan their responses to social situations. Game-playing helps children practice rules, learn strategies, and practice winning and losing.

Table 5: Social Domain (continued)

	Ages 2–4	Ages 5–7	Ages 8–9	Ages 10–11
Personal World	• Focused on self • Engage in parallel play	• Have friendships that are short-lived • Friendships based on interests	• Developing stable same-sex friendships • Friendships based on interests	• Understand friendship • Value loyalty and honesty • Have best friends
Related CE Activities	• Work in groups of two or three • Make cards for Christian holy days	• Work in groups of five or six • Focus groups on common work plan	• Participate in pageants and children's events	• Make short presentations to congregation
Self-Image	• Need adult assistance and assurance	• Enjoy new independence • Need adult assurance	• Egocentric • Overestimate skills and abilities	• Realistic self-assessment
Related CE Activities	• Teach songs that reinforce Christian self-image ("Jesus Loves Me," "Jesus Loves the Little Children") • Use Africentric religious materials	• Use and adapt Africentric religious materials • Bible stories about protection (the birth and rescue of Moses, Exodus 2)	• Use and adapt Africentric religious materials • Bible stories (Joseph and the coat of many colors, Genesis 37)	• Use and adapt Africentric religious materials • Africentric interpretation of Bible stories (The black man in Acts 8)

Techniques for Encouraging Christian Learning in Young and Elementary School Children

Organizing the Classroom

Classrooms for young learners should use tables (rectangular, round, or square) at which four children can sit facing one another and that

Table 6: Emotional Domain

	Ages 2–4	Ages 5–7	Ages 8–9	Ages 10–11
Emotional Development	• Act out emotions • Don't accurately label emotions • May have tantrums if upset • Respond to tangible reinforcement (praise, touch, stickers)	• Act out emotions • Label emotions • All or nothing thinkers • Short-term upsets, easily resolved • Respond to tangible reinforcement	• Label emotions accurately • May tease peers • Respond to tangible reinforcement	• Express themselves well • Communicate with facial expressions • Pride themselves on describing their feelings • Label the feelings of others • Respond to praise
Related CE Activities	• Games to label feelings • Learn Bible stories about Jesus as a child	• Learn Ten Commandments • Learn the Lord's Prayer	• Write and recite short poems about Christian behaviors • Write and recite Christian hip-hop songs	• Write and act in plays about Christian responses to current events, peer problems such as teasing, and relationships with parents, siblings, and peers

have surfaces that are sufficiently large for games and materials that will be used in activities. Organized classrooms provide structure that gives emotional comfort to young learners.

Choosing Age-Appropriate Materials
Sunday school and Vacation Bible School materials are designed to be appropriate to children at different stages of development. Christian educators wishing to design their own materials should evaluate resources at local bookstores. These resources should address teaching

Table 7: Intellectual Domain

	Ages 2–4	Ages 5–7	Ages 8–9	Ages 10–11
Intellectual Skills	• Learn simple rules • Practice new skills	• Learn more complex rules • Skills mastery (More interested in doing than creating) • Practice new skills	• Interested in projects • Interested in learning new things	• Interested in projects • Interested in creating and learning new things
Related CE Activities	• Do Africentric Christian arts and crafts • Learn and practice Christian songs	• Do Africentric Christian arts and crafts • Practice memory skills with verses, children's prayers	• Practice memory skills with verses, children's prayers, Ten Commandments • Draw familiar Bible stories • Do Africentric mapping activities	• Generate their own questions and answers • Develop personal prayers • Do Africentric mapping activities

to learning style, a child's level of development, and topics interesting to children that can be presented within a Christian framework.

Websites with Bible stories and age-appropriate activities that can be located on websites are identified throughout the chapter or at the end of this section. They can be used as is or adapted as appropriate.

Africentric Approaches

Africentric approaches are those that seek to infuse into all learning activities a philosophy of belief. This belief states that, in order to know who we are as children of God, we must learn and incorporate into our daily lives information that corrects the history lessons we are traditionally taught, encourages pride in self rather than the self-hatred that is likely to result from media presentations about us, identifies and supports strengths and talents, values and promotes education, and celebrates our collective contributions to the world that God made. The following methods assist the goal of creating an African-centered Christian teaching model:

Purchase Africentric materials. Available from many vendors, these materials are designed for African American children. They address issues important to the African American community, present ideas from an African American perspective, and use African American children and adults as models for photographs. See the references at the end of this section for the names of several African American Christian education resources.

Supply crayons in African-inspired flesh tones. It is now possible to purchase crayons that reflect the array of skin tones found among African Americans. These crayons allow children to draw accurate portraits of themselves, their families, their communities, and many of the Bible personalities they learn about in Christian education classes.

Draw Christian values. Give younger children the task of drawing pictures in which they are demonstrating adherence to Christian values ("Draw a picture illustrating respect (Matthew 7:12), obedience to parents (Ephesians 6:1), helping others (Luke 10:25-37), living a life that honors God (Micah 6:7-9), and other Christian values.") Have older children independently locate the Bible verses that match their drawings, an activity that will test their memory for the books of the Bible and memorized verses, and facilitate their use of a concordance to find additional verses that describe Christian attributes.

Discover the color of Jesus. Point out the birthplace of Jesus on a world map, help older children locate passages that describe the color of his skin and the texture of his hair (Revelation 1:12-16), and have them draw pictures of Jesus that can be placed on display in the church. Discuss why they see so few representations of Jesus as a black man.

Display Africentric art, magazines, and books. Seeing people who resemble you in art and literature boosts self-esteem. Africentric books are readily available at local black bookstores or from online booksellers. Portraits that depict Jesus as black are also available from a variety of sources. For example, the National Catholic Reporter conducted a contest for a portrait of Jesus for the national millennium celebration. Chosen from 1,500 entries from 1,000 artists in nineteen countries and six continents, the winner was "Jesus of the People," a black image painted by Vermont artist Janet McKenzie. It can be viewed at www.africana.com, www.natcath.com, or located by www.google.com (keywords: Catholic Reporter Black Jesus).

Conduct African-centered mapping activities. Using the Peters Projection map and the African American Jubilee Bible, or online mapping resources (see www.nationalgeographic.com) that teach about the land of Ham, re-learn the continent of Africa, and train children to understand the history of how African people and the Christian mission spread throughout the diaspora.

Identify God's glory in each child. Have children name people that they consider to be leaders and role models and discuss the leadership qualities their role models possess. Ask young learners to identify their own unique leadership qualities and to draw pictures of themselves as leaders. A useful Bible verse for this activity is Genesis 12:1-2.

Remind them that Jesus loves all the little children. Being Africentric is not a separatist activity. "Invariably, Christian education must intentionally seek to reach all races and ethnic backgrounds."[5] Children should be encouraged to explore a range of friendships with children who may have different cultural heritages because this is an expected Christian behavior and a form of realistic preparation for living in an increasingly multicultural society.

Celebrate Christmas the African American way. Of course, there is no one African American celebration tradition for Christmas. Children can learn, however, from hearing stories from members of the church who come from different celebration traditions. For example, Christian educators can ask church members from Africa, the Caribbean, and different portions of the United States to share with their church family stories, songs, and activities (crafts, games, and food preparation) related to their particular Christmas traditions.

Teach the values of Kwanzaa. Many African American churches now celebrate Kwanzaa after Christmas, viewing its values as consistent with Christian theology and its observance as a way to strengthen families, build communities, and celebrate culture. These values, called the Nguzo Saba, are listed in Chapter Two on page 19.

Explore specialty websites and products. Many websites are dedicated to providing excellent information that is meaningful to the lives of

African American Christians. See www.blackandchristian.com (history of African American churches, chat rooms, literature resources, and interesting articles) and www.africana.com (African American daily news and educational resources) as starting points for Web searches. Encarta Africana, the computer-based encyclopedia from which africana.com gets its information, is also available for purchase directly from Microsoft and vendors of computer supplies.

TEACHABLE MOMENT

Benjamin E. Mays Male Academy
Greater Christ Baptist Church, Detroit, Michigan

Many African American churches address specific Africentric teaching objectives by providing programs targeted to the specific learning needs of parishioners. Concerned about the status of black males in today's society, many churches have developed programs to provide boys with positive role models and have established rites of passage to teach traditions of responsible manhood.

Named after the African American educator, the Benjamin E. Mays Male Academy at the Greater Christ Baptist Church is a self-contained elementary school, grades K-5, that prepares young African American males to develop the academic and spiritual skills required for personal success and survival and potential contributions to the extended community. The Christian education component focuses on teaching Christian values rather than Christian dogma. These values are reinforced through the course of the day as the boys interact with each other, adult staff members, and their parents.

According to Academy founder Rev. James Perkins, the school was intentionally named for Dr. Mays, former Morehouse College president, "the consummate educator and molder and shaper of African American men. The name reflects a shared focus on Mays' Core Values: that racism is a reality but not an excuse. Rather, it is a reason to strive for excellence, doing this by preparing yourself with an education and presenting yourself with pride."

Rev. James Perkins, Senior Pastor, Greater Christ Baptist Church, telephone interviews and program materials, August 2002

Notes

1. Lora-Ellen McKinney. *www.eurekalearning.org (Case Study: Black Child Development Institute), accessed September 10, 2002.*

2. *Janice Hale and V. P. Franklin.* Learning While Black: Creating Educational Excellence for African American Children. *Baltimore: Johns Hopkins University Press, 2001, Foreword.*

3. *James Abbington, statement, 2002 Hampton University Ministers' Conference Choir Directors and Organist Guild Workshop, June 5, 2002.*

4. *Tables 4–7 were adapted from NNCC Developmentally Appropriate Planning for School Age Children, www.nncc.org, accessed September 10, 2002.*

5. *Elder Vincent Harrison, Senior Director of Education, New Birth Missionary Baptist Church, e-mail interview, September 6, 2002.*

CHAPTER SEVEN

HEART AND SOUL THEOLOGY

Effective Teaching and Learning
for Preteens and Teens

Lord, it's more than I'll ever understand,
how I am preserved by thy hand.
But then there's only two things required of me:
to be faithful (because I've been set free)
and so to be willing to be used by Thee.
So Lord I come willing to be used by Thee.[1]

THE MAIN TASK OF ADOLESCENCE IS INDEPENDENCE. THOUGH THEY
continue to have desires for recognition, success, approval, and parental
love, preteens (twelve-year-olds) and teenagers (ages thirteen to eighteen) are increasingly interested in being seen as capable people with
specific skills, interests, and abilities. Chief among those perceived
capacities is the ability to make their own decisions. Because they view
themselves as increasingly able to manage their own affairs, the teen
years are also characterized by emotional changes that result in their
wish for privacy, autonomy, and decreased dependence on their parents
for obvious emotional support. As part of their practice for true independence, teens tend to turn to each other for support and information.

African American teens have a number of social pressures not experienced by their non-black peers. Black boys who dress in the styles of
the day are likely to be viewed as dangerous, making them targets for
police and the objects of fear for shop owners, teachers, and many
other adults. Black girls, influenced in their dress and behavior by the
reigning songstresses of the moment, are often seen as sexual prey
though their bravado in style often masks an array of insecurities.

While part of the job of Christian educators is to work with parents whenever possible to establish rules for proper decorum, Christian educators are also charged with accepting God's children as they are and working with them to help them become all that Christ expects them to be. Finally, it is essential that Christian educators provide for African American children appropriate models of Christ-centered living, support, and affirmation for their efforts, and opportunities to be part of positive Christian communities that value each of them as unique contributing members.

The teen years are characterized by a number of changes:

Physical. Teenage bodies are taking on their adult form. They are reaching their full height, and, as a result of brain changes based on sex hormones that are preparing them for adult reproductive functions, their bodies are maturing. This is also a period of major brain growth and change, the first big change since the early childhood years. To function effectively, teenagers require lots of nutritious food and a considerable amount of sleep.[2]

Social. Teenagers enter new school systems where they must adjust to and function successfully in new academic environments that have more complicated schedules. They must operate in larger social environments, establish new friendships, and try new activities. Wanting to gain social acceptance, teenagers tend to function in groups. While these groups can provide meaningful support, they can also establish rules that are unfair, making the social aspect of the teen years a cycle of acceptance and rejection with the attendant emotions of joy and pain.

Emotional. As a result of friendship cycles and physical and hormonal changes, adolescence is an emotional time, one that many teens find confusing. Though they have many of the skills they will require as adults, they have not yet had enough experiences to properly judge many of the choices that are available to them.

Familial. Though often confusing and painful for parents, teen independence, experienced by parents as a loosening of the parent-child bond, is a necessary step. It is the teenagers' opportunity to test, within a supportive and loving environment, the skills they require to make lasting friendships, form relationships that may one day lead to marriage, identify personal strengths and weaknesses, effectively manage loss, and make good and bad choices, experiencing the benefits and consequences of each.

As we all can recall, adolescence is a chance for many things to go wrong. However, they are much less likely to go wrong if parents have established rules and laid a strong foundation of expected family and social behaviors, are consistent and fair disciplinarians, provide experiences that expose their children to new information and allow them to explore talents, and talk to their children about values they find important, whether or not the child appears to be listening. Using this positive approach is a tactic that allows teens to explore their developing selves in a manner more likely, on balance, to be positive.

While it is highly likely that teens involved in Christian education are members of families that are emotionally close and that have well-established Christian expectations, there are other teens who will independently seek Christ. Whether they can identify problems that they need help with, find the social atmosphere of the church and its programs appealing, or are looking to the church to provide structure for them, Christian educators must embrace them all and provide for them programs that are meaningful, interesting, fun, and challenging. For all teens involved in the church, Christian education is an important strategy for setting things right.

Goals of Christian Education for Preteens and Teens

The Christian education challenge for African American teenagers is to build on their independence and skills, giving them opportunities to problem-solve and apply Christian principles to their home and school experiences. The goals of Christian education for preteens and teens are to:

- Reinforce Christian beliefs and behavioral expectations
- Provide them with a social group built on positive Christian beliefs
- Build their self-confidence by providing them with a Christian community that recognizes and supports their talents
- Provide them with a safe place to discuss and problem-solve negative experiences, such as experiences with the low expectations of racist institutions

- Get them actively and creatively involved in all venues for Christian education
- Support parental goals for them or, when appropriate, act in a parenting role
- Allow them to make mistakes by equipping them with the knowledge that Christ loves them and that the church will support their positive efforts for change

Skills That Expert Christian Educators of Preteens and Teens Bring to Their Classes

Christian educators of preteens and teens must:

Listen. Teens sort out their ideas and issues as they talk. Christian educators who talk more than they listen will miss important information and essential opportunities for teaching and for intervention.

Be non-judgmental. Though Christ has plans for our lives, we all stumble along the way. As we provide teens with Christian guidelines it is important to remind them that each mistake is an opportunity to learn and to make changes in the way that they live.

Be creative. Teens have short attention spans and lots of media competing for their attention. Christian educators must use teaching materials, including technology, in interesting ways so that teens remain interested and engaged.

Expect to learn. Things change. Each generation's youth have different stresses and pressures than the one that preceded them. No matter how confused Christian educators may be about the values and behaviors of today's youth, they will learn how to reach youth by observing them in social situations, listening to learn what they find important, watching what they purchase as a sign of what they value, seeing how they behave with different people and in different settings, and hearing the messages that lie behind their words.

Know how to have fun. Fun is an essential part of life for all human beings. Christian education cannot be a dry, boring enterprise. Find out what teens like to do and do with them those things that will be enjoyable and meet their objectives for Christian growth.

Remember your youth. Teenagers can be frustrating. We can increase our patience by remembering how we behaved (or thought about behaving) when we were younger.

Principles of Development and Learning for Preteens and Teens (Ages 12–18)

In the middle school and high school years, adolescents are focused on independence, body image, personal interests, intellectual pursuits, sexuality, rules and limit testing, selection of role models, trying to fit in to social settings, and experimenting with new personas (changing hairstyles and clothing). Most teens are tempted to experiment with lifestyles as well—use of drugs and alcohol and first sexual experiences tend to occur during the teen years. This is also a time when teenagers seek, though often in subtle ways, reinforcement for what they have learned from parents and teachers. Many of the stereotypical negative teen behaviors can be avoided by creating environments that encourage discussion, listening to what is unsaid, and actively providing support for positive efforts and behaviors.

Teenagers learn best when their:

Ideas are valued. Teenagers worry about being disrespected by peers and misunderstood by adults. It is important to them that their ideas are heard and discussed in meaningful ways.

Contributions are recognized. Teens exhibit a range of social behaviors as they manage this time of changes in all aspects of their development. Some teens will approach life boldly, while others will feel uncertain of themselves. Christian educators can assist both groups by encouraging their active participation in activities and discussions, acknowledging their statements and accomplishments, and providing ways for their talents to be used in Christian education venues.

Perspectives are placed in broader contexts. Though they have many interesting ideas and increasingly more experiences, teenagers tend to be very centered on themselves and are not easily able to take the perspective of others (this is why they often make bad choices). It is important for Christian educators to introduce teens to new ideas so that their views will be based on accurate information and the needs of others rather than on emotion and personal self-interest.

Table 8

	Ages 12–13	Ages 14–16	Ages 17–18
Physical Development	• Feel awkward about body's physical changes	• Clear physical maturation • Increased comfort with physical changes	• Some growth spurts • Firmer sense of sexual identity • Strong sensual interests
Related CE Activities	• Reinforcement of rules for appropriate church dress • Liturgical dance, drama, and ministry participation • Group recreational activities	• Reinforcement of rules for appropriate church dress • Liturgical dance, drama, and ministry participation • Group recreational activities	• Reinforcement of rules for appropriate church dress • Liturgical dance, drama, and ministry participation • Group recreational activities
Social Domain	• Interests influenced by peers • Frequently changing relationships • Limit testing	• Concern with attractiveness to others • Improved ability to express personal views • Limit-testing with adults • Pull back from parents	• Social and family traditions regain importance • Concern with personal dignity and respect
Related CE Activities	• Group activities and controlled competitions • Youth ministries (e.g. choir, usher board) • Volunteer for church ministries and community projects	• Group projects and activities • Youth ministries (e.g. choir, usher board) • Volunteer for church ministries and community projects	• Youth-led group discussions • Youth ministries (e.g. choir, usher board) • Design and implement volunteer activities • Learn about Africans in the diaspora

	Ages 12–13	Ages 14–16	Ages 17–18
Emotional Domain	• Worry about being accepted • Shift role models • Need immediate gratification	• Struggle with sense of identity • Identify parental faults • Seek role models	• Recognize parental imperfections • Experience feelings of love • Can better delay gratification • Prepare to leave home for work or college
Related CE Activities	• Rites of Passage training and celebration • Special role in all church events	• Small-group discussions based on current events • Special role in all church events	• Write and produce dramas on important teen issues • Special role in all church events
Intellectual Domain	• Interested in the present • Well-defined skills • Increased attention span	• Capacity for abstract thought • Plan for the future • Increased ability to take the perspective of others • Develop ideals • More stable work habits	• Think about their life purpose • Consider vocations • Set personal goals • Interest in moral reasoning • Self-motivated task completion
Related CE Activities	• Solo or group musical, oratory, or dramatic presentations	• Sunday school assistance with younger children • Write teen column for church website or newsletter • Mapping activities	• Leadership in worship • Involvement in college preparation ministries • Mapping activities

Techniques for Encouraging Christian Learning in Preteens and Teens

Organize the Classroom

Classrooms organized in circular form provide face-to-face contact that facilitates appropriate social interaction and increases maximum group involvement for teenagers. Teens also enjoy decorating their classrooms, assisting their teachers with tasks, doing computer-based research, and designing graphic materials.

Choose Age-appropriate Materials and Activities

Africentric religious publishers of Sunday school and other training materials have books, magazines, and activities appropriate to the learning needs and interests of younger and older teens (see references at the end of the section). Using Africentric and Christian website materials and locating relevant books, videos, CDs, DVDs, and materials in local bookstores are other options for finding materials that will capture teen interest.

Utilize Africentric Approaches

Teens may enjoy the following activities as ways of making personal and group contributions to a church's ministry:

Research the Lord's web. Have teens select a topic that is of Christian interest and conduct research on it on African-centered websites such as www.blackandchristian.com, www.Africana.com, www.gospelnet.com, or sites that they locate independently.

Share the drama with your mama. Teens enjoy opportunities to share their worldviews. Work with them on developing dramatic productions that illustrate Christian themes, apply Christian principles to teen dilemmas, and celebrate the contributions of African Americans. Identify church members who are skilled at set design, sewing, script writing and editing, vocal projection and control, musicianship, and acting to serve as consultants for youth drama projects.

Dance like the ancestors. African peoples have often developed dances to celebrate important life events. Locate persons in the congregation or local community who are knowledgeable about African dance and work with youth to create liturgical dances based on African themes and African dance styles.

Go Hollywood. Provide disposable cameras for students (or have them use family cameras) to photograph God's handiwork in interesting ways. Many computers include movie-making software that can turn still photos, aided by student voiceovers and audio additions from the youth choir, into movies to share with the congregation.

Teach life strategies. Racism continues to exist in the world, and, as a result, some of the best gifts Christian educators and parents can give to African American youth are support of excellence in all of their endeavors as a tool for fighting low expectations.

Learn the traditions of Christmases past. Preteens and teens are interested in learning from their elders when information is presented in a manner that they can easily relate to. *A Treasury of African American Christmas Stories* by Bettye Collier-Thomas is a book that shares Christmas stories and traditions from 1890 to 1915, stories that can be read and discussed or turned into stage productions for a Christmas pageant (see resource list at the end of the section).

Praise him with the psalter. Develop a youth music ministry that teaches youth to play musical instruments. Teach youth to play traditional and modern musical pieces from the *African American Heritage Hymnal* (GIA Publications, 2001), to learn the works of black secular composers (www.google.com, keyword: black composers), and those of modern African American religious composers such as Glenn Burleigh, Kirk Franklin, Richard Smallwood, Nolan Williams, and others. Musical training of this sort provides a wonderful addition to the music ministry of the church, teaches an important skill, and provides a creative avenue for learning self-discipline.

Notes

1. *Genna Rae McNeil, "Lord I'm Willing (1989)," in James Melvin Washington, Ph.D, editor.* Conversations with God: Two Centuries of Prayers by African Americans. *New York: HarperCollins Publishers, 1994, page 256.*

2. *New research has actually led to policy changes in many high schools around the country. These schools start around 10 a.m. because research on teen brain behavior has indicated that adolescents don't function well early in the morning.*

WALKING IN THE WORD

Effective Teaching and Learning for Adults

No matter how full the river, it still wants to grow.[1]

ADULTS REQUIRE TEACHING STYLES THAT ACCOMMODATE THEIR existing knowledge and experiences. Whether they are young adults (ages eighteen to twenty-one) or more mature adults (over age twenty-one) they have typically spent a considerable amount of time in structured learning environments that have provided them with information and taught them what teaching strategies work best for them. Young adults are at decision points in their lives, determining whether to attend college or enter the work force. Mature adults have also spent time in the work world and, in each work experience, have gained insight into the skills and information they require to do well on their jobs. They have experience in relationships and may also be parents, experiences that inform their interests and viewpoints. Finally, they have had the time to put many aspects of their lives into perspective and to have identified and hopefully learned from their past mistakes and missteps.

Adult learning requirements are based on their preferred learning styles (see Chapter Five) and a wish to understand new materials within the context of their personal experiences. While there are few well-established theories that address adult learners as a unique group in their learning styles, adults are likely to have several sets of personal learning goals:

Subject-oriented learning. Adults may wish to master specific content. In the case of Christian education, they may wish to learn how to be better stewards of the resources that God has given to them. If they are new Christians, they may wish to more fully understand the commitment they have made and are likely to dedicate their learning goals to basic facts about Christian beliefs.

Learning that produces life changes. For many adults, the decision to learn something new reflects a wish to enhance the quality of their lives, to gain new skills that can result in better employment or completion of academic processes previously set aside.

Self-guided learning. Adult learners often wish to direct the course of their learning, acting as full participants in any learning process. In Christian education courses, some adults will wish to use the time to explore materials and engage in discussions about issues that are important to their Christian journey.

Christian educators who work with adult learners can anticipate learners who are motivated, opinionated, specific about their learning goals, and excited about participating in an experience that will provide them with life-changing information.

Teaching Young Adults

Understand this developmental stage. Young adults, those who have graduated from high school into college or the workforce, bring to Christian education a perception of themselves as productive, functioning members of society. Often they wish to be active participants in learning and to have available to them a range of course options.

Teach life strategies. Young adults are learning basic life skills. It is important for them to know how to balance a checkbook, how to plan their budgets, how to save for desired items and activities, and strategies for being effective employees, spouses, and parents. Christian education stewardship courses can greatly aid young adults in developing the skills required to manage the resources that God has shared with them. Courses on Christian relationship development and parenting can provide a framework for the future planning and building of strong families based on Christian principles.

Develop leadership. To keep young adults involved in the life of the church and to create a pipeline through which young leaders can emerge, departments of Christian education should consider providing leadership training courses as a standard requirement for those who seek to lead ministries. Christian leadership courses can lead to a certificate and can include courses on theology, stewardship, and the pastoral vision for church growth and development.

Teaching Mature Adults

Vary teaching styles. Many types of learners will show up in every venue for Christian education. Because their attendance and participation in Christian education is voluntary, Christian educators must work to create vibrant learning experiences that address the learning styles, needs, and goals of a number of learners.

- Lectures should be brief, followed by a period of time that provides for meaningful questions and answers.
- Workshops should provide information desired by learners, present new facts, and facilitate discussions that aid participants in applying principles to their lives.
- Small-group activities allow adult learners to focus intensely on learning new information and, in discussions with a few other persons, sharing relevant life experiences.

In each setting, Christian educators can provide desired information, ask questions in a manner that encourages active participation and approach the teaching task that facilitates discovery of new aspects of God's Word.

Ask open-ended questions. Questions that encourage brief responses and yes or no answers stifle creativity and interest.

Sit in a circle. Except in lectures, a circular seating arrangement allows all participants to see one another, encouraging the building of relationships within the Christian community. It also places the teacher in the position of facilitator, one that is less likely to be perceived as imbued with all-knowing power. The Christian educator can, in this way, be relieved from the burden of "expert" expectations and can feel freer to be a well-informed learner.

Share leadership. So that everyone has an opportunity for full participation in Christian education activities, participants can take turns providing opening and closing prayer, sharing passages of Scripture, and making topical presentations each week.

Teaching Senior Saints

While the motivations for adult learning hold true throughout our life-times, the aging process does affect adult learning in very specific ways. In older adults, usually persons age sixty-five and over (though changes often start much earlier):

- Intellectual capabilities tend to decline
- Hearing and vision decrease (beginning at age forty and forty-five, respectively)
- Attention to detail creates challenges for taking in and retrieving information
- There is decreased memory for new information, though early memories remain intact
- Physical abilities and response times become slower
- Learning new skills can be difficult and can take more time unless they are learned in the context of familiar schemes
- Vocabulary and highly practiced and expert behaviors change less than other skills

Based on age-based learning differences, Christian education for older adults should:

Teach to typical learning styles. Even though older adults are experiencing physiological changes and shifts in learning behaviors, they still have learning sense preferences. Seniors maintain their preferences for auditory, visual, kinesthetic, and relational teaching approaches. (See Chapter Five.)

Use amplification. Even those who have hearing aids greatly benefit from lessons presented in loud, clear voices.

Provide visual aids. Most adults over the age of forty-five require magnification to see well. Overheads, PowerPoint presentations, and large-print handouts are helpful to those whose vision is changing.

Allow processing time. Because seniors may require more time to process information, it is essential that Christian educators move through programs and classes at an adjusted pace. Class members will let educators know what pace is comfortable.

Encourage storytelling. Seniors have amazing stories from their lives that they can share to provide examples of facing challenges successfully, living for Christ, and dealing with adversity. Earlier memories are frequently stronger than more recent ones, so it is important to encourage seniors to share stories of their choosing.

Respect your elders. Senior church members have lived lives filled with experience. Even if their personalities change as they get older, younger Christian educators must be respectful of them, encourage their perspectives, and engage them in programs and processes with learners of all ages.

Prepare shorter lessons. Because older people may process information more slowly over time, Christian educators should prepare shorter lessons and expect discussions to move more slowly.

Accommodate physical limitations. Some older persons have physical limitations and frailties that should be accommodated in classrooms and in church ministries and activities. Church facilities should have comfortable chairs in classrooms and room in facility spaces for walking aids such as canes, walkers, and wheelchairs. See Chapter Nine for information about ways to provide ministries for persons with physical limitations and disabilities.

Be patient. One day, God willing, you too will be an interesting, experienced, and valued senior saint.

Africentric Approaches

A visit with the elders. People of African descent have traditionally valued the wisdom that comes with age. Organize a churchwide activity that creates an African village and the activities likely to take place within it. (Conduct research on www.nationalgeographic.com, www.encarta.com, and in the African American Jubilee Edition of the Holy Bible—see Section One resources—to determine village design and traditions.) As one activity, provide a tent where the village elders can share with those who seek their counsel about the skills, beliefs, and behaviors required for success in life. Have their words recorded for use in a story to be placed in the church newsletter (see Archival Activities on page 123) or the church website to assure that those who cannot attend the event can also learn from the life experience of the church's senior saints.

Discover the diaspora. Many African American adults are unfamiliar with African history in the Christian mission, with the travel paths by which Africans moved to different parts of the world (independently or for slavery), and with the places where persons of African descent currently reside in large numbers. The following activities may be useful for adult learners.

- Study the history of the Africans in biblical history. *Africans Who Shaped Our Faith* (citation is found in Section One references) provides sermons, scripture references, and study questions on ten Africans in the Bible. Use reading materials and study guides found in the African American Jubilee Bible to assist personal and group study.
- Learn to defend the faith. Many books, including several by Usry and Keener (listed in Section One references) provide answers to common questions about African American Christianity.
- Find a whole new world. Use the Peters Projection maps and maps located in the African American Jubilee Bible that accurately portray the proportions of the African continent and note places of import to the Afri-Christian story.
- Partner with your people. Become partners with a church in Africa, Brazil, or the Caribbean. Facilitate this connection by using denominational foreign mission societies as resources.
- Travel to the homeland. Travel to Africa or other parts of the African diaspora with Christian travel groups. Consolidated Tours of Atlanta (404-767-2727) organizes many tours for African American church groups.

Note

1. *African proverb. Charlotte and Wolf Lesau, compilers.* African Proverbs. *White Plains, New York: Peter Pauper Press, 1985, page 17.*

IS THERE A WORD FROM THE LORD?

Christian Education for Special Needs Populations[1]

When I said yes to Jesus, life became new; I then realized that God had really worked miraculously in me.[2]

JESUS LOVES ALL OF HIS CHILDREN AND WANTS THEM TO HAVE ACCESS to his message. Ministries for special needs populations are a unique opportunity for African American churches to include all church members in Christian education, to provide meaningful emotional and practical support for families, to actively demonstrate the expansive love of God, and to learn lessons and receive blessings that we might otherwise miss. More than providing a special service, ministries to special needs populations should be viewed as experiences that empower them to become active members of the body of Christ and that create mutual learning experiences that, in turn, have an impact on the lives and learning experiences of all church members.

Goals for Ministries for Special Needs Populations

Ministries that address the needs of the deaf, blind, learning disabled, emotionally distressed, or physically challenged must be respectful of the learning styles and comfort needs of these members. Christian education programs must be inclusive, creating opportunities for active participation in all learning venues. Important goals for special-needs population ministries are to:

- Assess congregational needs so that the programs that are developed are relevant to parishioners and likely to be well utilized

- Provide high quality, accessible, and meaningful Christian education experiences for all church members
- Encourage the active participation of all church members in worship and Christian education activities
- Integrate individuals with special needs into all church programs, ministries, and classes
- Provide, when appropriate, classes dedicated to the specific learning needs of individuals with special needs
- Increase pastoral and congregational sensitivities to the contributions that disabled church members make to quality worship and Christian education experiences
- Eliminate barriers between people with "disabilities" and those who are not similarly challenged
- Employ disabled church members, providing them with resources that will assist them in doing their jobs well
- Recognize that Jesus loves us all equally
- Create a church-wide learning environment

Ministries for Special Needs Populations

God calls us to reach out to all of our members and to reach out to those who require love and support. While all of us are included in the category of those who need the support of the Christian community to aid our development, some members of our congregations require additional practical support. Inclusion of special needs populations into Christian education reflects a shared congregational value, a commitment to service to others, and a wish to expand the boundaries of our relationships.

Churches that wish to increase their commitment to persons with disabilities will find it necessary to assess the needs of their particular congregation, individualize services where appropriate, assure comfortable access to church facilities, address the different learning needs of adults and children with disabilities, provide training for staff and Christian educators, and seek consultation from those experienced with ministering to deaf, blind, physically handicapped, emotionally distressed, or learning disabled church members.

Learning Styles and Needs of Special Needs Populations

In most cases, teaching strategies for special needs populations will not differ significantly from those described for auditory, visual, kinesthetic, and relational learning styles described in Chapter Five.

Persons with disabilities may require changes to activity rules, adaptations to time allotments, modifications to make activities more or less challenging, or the availability of special equipment (tables, chairs, eating utensils, cutting implements) so that disabled members can participate fully in Christian education programs. Many congregations will have members who, as family members or resulting from professional training, will be skilled at working with people with a variety of disabling conditions. Based on the severity of the disabling condition, churches might consider hiring or seeking volunteer teachers with special education experience.

TEACHABLE MOMENT

Assessing Congregational Needs for Special Services
ACCESS Ministry, McLean Bible Church, Vienna, Virginia

Each summer the McLean Bible Church provides a summer camp experience—including music, games, artwork, drama, recreation, and life skills—for school-aged children with special needs. Provided by the church's ACCESS Ministry, which has made a deliberate effort to provide Christian education services for members with special needs, the program gathers a range of information to ensure child safety and programmatic success. Parents of special needs campers are asked to complete a comprehensive form that seeks the following information: child's name; family information (names and ages of siblings, parent names and employment); camper height and weight; specific diagnosis (checklist provided) noting severity (mild, moderate, profound); communication needs; dietary and feeding needs; medications taken; doctor's name and phone numbers; allergies; needed medical precautions; toilet and hygiene needs; restrictions, if appropriate, for outdoor activities; and recommendations regarding the level of adult assistance each child requires to ensure safety and meaningful participation in the program.

Not intended to be exhaustive in the information they provide, the following recommendations for ministry development and support for special needs populations of church members can assist churches in thinking through how to provide services that include, value, respect, and accommodate the special needs of their members.

Recommendations for Creating and Supporting a Successful Deaf Ministry

Get everyone involved. Have the entire congregation learn to sign songs and prayers that occur weekly in worship services (for example, The Lord's Prayer, the Apostles' Creed, and specific praise songs).

Incorporate deaf persons into worship, classes, and programs. Include deaf persons in church activities by signing Scripture as it is read aloud, signing songs as the choir sings, or participating in a signing choir.

Make arrangements for members of deaf communities to attend worship. Because some deaf members may not drive, churches should provide transportation to and from worship, classes, and programs for those who need this service.

Provide dedicated seating for deaf members. They can sit together in a place where they can easily see interpreters. Though deaf members will benefit from feeling the presence of a deaf community within the congregation, hearing members should sit among them to practice signing and to learn better ways to communicate effectively with deaf members.

Encourage sign language study. Provide courses for those who are interested in becoming sign language interpreters for worship and classes.

Use technology effectively. Many churches have large screens that project worship services. They can be used to:

- Teach the congregation the signs that accompany songs and prayers
- Have the worship service signed or close captioned on a split screen
- Provide words to songs, prayers, and Scripture so that deaf members can easily follow along.

For churches that don't have this technology available, some deaf ministries use handouts.

Research available resources. Major bookstores and the Internet provide a variety of resources on deaf ministry development. Some websites provide materials appropriate to the learning needs of deaf members. Sign language coloring books can be found at www.deafadventist.org, and Christian resources and links for deaf ministries are featured on www.wholesomewords.org.

TEACHABLE MOMENT

Silent Mission
Shiloh Baptist Church, Washington, D.C.

One of the most moving things that I have ever seen is the work of our Silent Mission, a sign language interpretation ministry for the deaf. To raise consciousness and highlight the work of the Mission we taught the entire congregation to sign the doxology. We sign it every Sunday now.

Rev. George Mensah, Director of Christian Education,
Shiloh Baptist Church, telephone interview, August 5, 2002

Recommendations for Creating and Supporting a Successful Ministry for Visually Impaired Members

Provide transportation to worship and other Christian education offerings. Blind and visually impaired parishioners require transportation services to get to church. It is important to be punctual.

Build an audio library. Include Christian books on tape and other audio-tape and CD resources as part of a lending library available to blind and visually impaired members.

Use large print. Provide large print books, Bibles, and church programs and newsletters for the visually impaired.

Provide Braille signs. Make it easier for blind members to know their location in church buildings by identifying elevators, floors, and facility rooms with Braille signs.

Ask permission to touch. Ask blind and visually impaired members if they require assistance and their preference for that assistance (letting them hold your arm as they cross the street, for example), and gain their permission to enter their personal space through touch.

Fight loneliness. Blindness sometimes leads to a sense of isolation. Include blind members in social activities at the church and in the homes of other members. Enhance relational learning by holding Bible study with sighted and blind members, reading the Bible aloud to create a shared experience of God's Word.

Don't touch guide dogs. Guide dogs are not pets in the traditional sense. When accompanying their masters, they are working and should not be distracted from their duties and routine.

Research available resources. Major bookstores and the Internet provide a variety of resources on blind ministry development as well as books, hymnals, and educational materials written in Braille. Some websites provide resources appropriate to the learning needs of blind members (online newsletter, evangelism strategies and training opportunities—www.namb.net; Christian resources and links for ministries for the blind and visually impaired—www.careministries.org; Baptist Braille hymnals—www.blindsight-ministries.com).

Recommendations for Creating and Supporting a Successful Ministry for Members with Orthopedic Impairments
Be accessible.

- Ramp and bathroom accommodations. In compliance with the Americans with Disabilities Act of 1990, new construction must include ramps and accessible bathroom facilities, and older facilities must be retrofitted to meet these requirements. Even if your church meets the basic requirements of the law, be sure to ask disabled members (or their family members when appropriate) if the accommodations are sufficient and seek their input on improvements.

- Classrooms. Classrooms should have doors wide enough to accommodate wheelchairs and special equipment. Classrooms may also need tables and workstations that can be adjusted to accommodate equipment and provide stable sources of physical support.

- Sanctuary. The sanctuary should have an area where people in wheelchairs, on crutches, and using other equipment can sit without blocking aisles or violating fire codes.

Provide transportation. Churches can purchase special vans or develop relationships with accessible public transportation services to provide comfortable rides to and from church services, Sunday school classes, Christian education activities, and church social events.

Individualize activities. Each person with orthopedic impairments and other physical disabilities has a different set of skills and abilities. Be sensitive to individual needs.

Research available resources. Major bookstores and the Internet provide a variety of resources on ministry for physically disabled child and adult church members. Some websites provide resources appropriate to the learning and accommodation needs of physically handicapped members (disability directory for National Church Ministries—www.cmalliance.org; Seventh Day Adventist Church—http://.nadadvantist.org/humanrelations).

Recommendations for Creating and Supporting a Successful Ministry for Learning (Cognitively) Disabled Members

Understand the range of cognitive disabilities. People with cognitive disabilities are unable to process information that they see, hear, and experience in age-appropriate ways.

Understand the causes of cognitive disabilities. Cognitive disabilities, all of which impact learning capacities, can arise from genetic conditions or can be caused by trauma such as accidents, illness, or abuse. A range of labels describes very different cognitive challenges, among which are learning disabilities, developmental disabilities, mental retardation, Down syndrome, and autism.

Don't limit your perception of your students. Though cognitively disabled learners have obvious limitations, they also have skills that they bring to any learning environment. They should be encouraged to participate to the best of their ability in church activities. A mentally retarded adult, for example, may function at the level of a twelve-year-old. Those who have been parents of twelve-year-olds understand that they have lots of abilities and the capacity to bring joy to their community of friends and family.

Use prompts, reminders, and cues. Learners with cognitive disabilities may require reminders about the purpose of an activity and subtle and obvious cues that "jumpstart" a process. The first line of The Lord's

Prayer or traditional songs, for example, may serve as a reminder of the sequence of words and phrases.

Vary the sensory format of activities. Because information can be challenging to process quickly, it is important to teach to a variety of learning styles and to use in each teaching situation an assortment of learning tools. Activities and approaches used for kinesthetic learners can be especially helpful. See Chapter Five for information on learning styles and related teaching approaches.

Research available resources. Major bookstores and the Internet provide a variety of resources on strategies for teaching persons with cognitive and developmental disabilities. Cognitive and developmental disabilities resources are available online at www.waisman.wisc.edu.

Recommendations for Creating and Supporting a Successful Ministry for Emotionally Ill or Distressed Members

Understand the reasons for mental illness. All congregations have members who have or will have emotional problems. Some may have short-term problems that result from difficult emotional experiences such as the events of September 11, 2001, and the unexpected loss of loved ones, while others become mentally ill as a result of brain chemical imbalances.

Be sensitive to the many faces of emotional distress. Many church members are clinically depressed, involved in abusive relationships, recovering from the abuse of alcohol and drugs, and struggling with negative self-perceptions as a result of childhood experiences of family dysfunction including physical, emotional, and sexual abuse. In determining lesson content and statements made in Christian education venues, educators should expect that someone in their hearing is in emotional distress and, as a consequence, must use language that respects personal circumstances.

Make Christian counseling resources available to church members. These services are available in many communities, perhaps even as a ministry of your own church. Through use of adaptations to traditional psychological treatment techniques, Christian counseling offers Christ's love and reminders of our status as worthy children of God.

Research available resources. Major bookstores and the Internet provide a variety of resources on ministry for physically disabled child and adult church members. Comprehensive online mental health resources are available at www.mental-health-matters.com.

Benefit of Specialized Programs for the Entire Congregation

God loves all of his children and wants them all to have access to his Word. Provision of special ministries requires a strong commitment on the part of pastor and parishioners to engage the Great Commission in a holistic manner.

Notes

1. *There are constantly changing conventions for terms used to describe persons with disabilities. The decision of this author was to employ terms most commonly used, with no intent to offend or misuse language in describing deaf, blind, cognitively disabled, emotionally distressed, and physically challenged populations.*

2. *Dr. Ruth Maness, "He Lives in Me," in Rev. Dr. Suzan Johnson Cook, editor,* Sister Strength: A Collection of Devotions for and from African American Women. *Nashville: Thomas Nelson Publishers, 1998, page 59.*

Top Ten Tips for Teaching Christian Education to Learners of All Ages and Ability Levels

1. View yourself as a facilitator of Christian learning.

2. Build relationships that enhance the learning processes of individuals and groups within the church.

3. Understand the characteristics of learning styles and teach to them.

4. Explore how the brain learns and incorporate this knowledge into your teaching approach.

5. Make Christian education an exciting experience for learners of all ages and ability levels.

6. Connect learners to Christ through explorations of his movement in the lives of African Americans.

7. Develop leadership from the ranks of learners in the church's many venues for Christian education.

8. Be honest about what you know and don't know.

9. Believe the blessings inherent in Christian education that embrace the special Christian education needs of church members with disabilities and other challenges.

10. Identify sources of information that enhance your capacity to understand unfamiliar issues and meet a wide variety of learning needs.

Preparation for the Journey

1. How must I prepare my department of Christian education to reach learners of all ages?

2. What special training and accommodations does my church require to meet the Christian education needs of church members with cognitive and physical disabilities, as well as for those with conditions, such as blindness and deafness, that require specialized forms of teaching and presentation?

3. What additional information regarding brain behavior do my staff and I require to best design programs for learners of different ages, developmental stages, learning styles, and ability levels?

4. What is my learning style? What adjustments must I make to my most comfortable learning style to better accommodate learners I have responsibility for teaching?

5. How can I use information on learning styles to improve teaching strategies and materials used in Christian education in my church?

6. What resources exist in my local community to help train Christian education staff to provide excellent African-centered Christian education to all members?

7. What strategies must I use to create a Christian religious community in my local church?

BASIC TEACHING SKILLS AND LEARNING STRATEGIES

Christian Education Teaching Tools

Stan Campbell and James S. Bell, Jr. *The Complete Idiot's Guide to the Bible.* Alpha Books: A Pearson Education Company, 1999. The authors provide summaries and interpretations of the contents of the Old and New Testaments, as well as interesting facts about the people, cities, and familiar stories found in the Bible. From it "you'll learn all about patriarchs and matriarchs, kings and kingdoms, prophets and losses, and the good news of Jesus Christ."

Bettye Collier-Thomas. *A Treasury of African American Christian Stories.* New York: Henry Holt and Company, 1997. These stories are grounded in the historical experiences of African Americans based on storytelling traditions. This book of stories focuses on issues and dilemmas that faced blacks between the years 1890 and 1915.

Israel Galindo. *The Craft of Christian Teaching: Essentials for Becoming a Very Good Teacher.* Valley Forge: Judson Press, 1998. This book presents a mode for understanding the uniqueness of Christian education, appropriate approaches for teaching Christian education, styles of learning that impact faith, and teaching skills that create effective instruction in church settings.

Kenneth O. Gangel and Howard G. Hendricks (Editors). *The Christian Educator's Handbook on Teaching.* Grand Rapids, Michigan: Baker Book House, 1998. Considered a comprehensive resource on Christian teaching, this book discusses the foundations of Christian teaching, teaching different age groups, teaching different social groups (families, church, and community), and the Christian educator as a teacher, maker of disciples, and student of the Bible.

Josh McDowell. *The New Evidence That Demands a Verdict: Evidence I and II Fully Updated in One Volume to Answer Questions Challenging Christians in the 21st Century.* Nashville:

Thomas Nelson Publishers, 1999. Providing an amazing array of research-based facts useful for teaching, this book answers, among many others, questions about the historical reliability of the information in the Old and New Testaments and the meaning and uses of the divine names of God. It addresses Christian controversies (for example, whether the Resurrection was a hoax or is historical fact) and provides ground rules for assessing these issues.

Josh McDowell and Don Stewart. *Answers to Tough Questions Skeptics Ask About the Christian Faith.* Carol Stream, Illinois: Tyndale House Publishers, 1986. Available in English and Spanish, this book tackles sixty-five of the most-asked questions about the Bible, God, Jesus Christ, miracles, other religions, and Creation in a question-and-answer format.

Effective Teaching Strategies

Children and Teenagers

Janice Hale-Benson. *Black Children: Their Roots, Culture and Learning Style.* Baltimore: Johns Hopkins University Press, 1986. Known for designing schools whose goal was the facilitation of intelligence in black children, this book focuses on explaining the emotive and relational learning styles of black children. It provides specific information on effective teaching strategies and validates the unique manner in which the black experience impacts the more traditional assessment of learning styles.

Janice Hale and V. P. Franklin. *Learning While Black: Creating Educational Excellence for African American Children.* Baltimore: Johns Hopkins University Press, 2001. As educators who understand the role of the church in the lives of African Americans, these authors discuss learning styles and the impact of African American church on providing experiences that enrich the lives of its children.

Neil McQueen. *Computer, Kids and Christian Education: How to Use Computers in Your Christian Education Program.* Minneapolis, Minnesota: Augsburg Fortress Publishers, 2001. Based on the premise that "one of the most important things a church can do for its children is to reach into the culture and redeem the tools that children are exposed to and using in their everyday world for Christ's sake," this book provides Christian education teachers with practical tools that enhance teaching.

Adults

Kathleen Taylor, Catherine Marienau, and Morris Fiddler. *Cognitive Styles and Learning Strategies: Developing Adult Learners.* New York: John Wiley, 2000. Though this book was developed for those who teach adults in continuing education and other settings, it provides useful tools that Christian educators can apply for use in their classes.

Bruce H. Wilkinson. *How to Teach Almost Anything to Practically Anyone: The 7 Laws of the Learner Series.* Sisters, Oregon: Multnomah Publishers, Inc., 1992. Wilkinson focuses on techniques for teaching that create not just new learning but also life changes.

Special Needs Populations

Elaine Costello. *Religious Signing: A Comprehensive Guide for All Faiths.* New York: Bantam Books, 1986. This book describes the importance of sign language interpretation in worship and provides pictorial descriptions of signs for terms used in most worship services.

David A. Sousa. *How the Special Needs Brain Learns.* Thousand Oaks, California: Corwin Press, 2001. This book addresses strategies for working effectively with children with a variety of disabilities.

Other Learning Models

Bernice McCarthy. *The 4MAT System: Teaching to Learning Styles with Right Left Mode Techniques.* Barrington, Illinois: Excel, Inc., 1987. This book is focused on teaching to learning styles (analytic, common sense, dynamic, and imaginative) as well as to the sense represented by each (thinking, doing, sensing feeling, and watching).

Other Christian Education Tools

PLACE: Finding Your Place in Ministry. PLACE stands for Personality Blends, Learning Spiritual Gifts, Abilities, Connecting Passion to Ministry, and Experiences in Life. This tool helps Christians identify their strengths and passions so that they can effectively match them with a church ministry and become actively engaged in it. PLACE can be ordered from MDC Today, P.O. Box 663, Oklahoma City, Oklahoma 73170, 877-463-2863, or www.placeministries.org. (Accessed September 10, 2002.)

Christian Education Websites

Beliefnet, **www.beliefnet.com.** The largest online multi-faith site provides information on comparative religions and many other resources (class meditations, prayer circles, and religious quizzes) that can be adapted for use in Christian education classes. (Accessed on September 10, 2002.)

Bibles.Net, **www.bibles.net.** This site is considered the Internet's most comprehensive resources for online biblical reference materials. It provides a concordance and the capacity to search for verses by topic in a number of Bible translations and versions, as well as in a variety of languages. (Accessed on September 10, 2002.)

Children's Bible Resources, **www.letusteachkids.com.** This site provides tools for children's ministry including stories, newsletters, teacher training materials, child appropriate Bible stories, and dramatic and puppetry resources. (Accessed on September 10, 2002.)

DiscipleLand, **www.discipleland.com.** This site has Christian education materials for use with children ages two to fourteen aimed at helping them reach their full potential in Christ by equipping them for effective discipleship. (Accessed on September 10, 2002.)

Gospel Communications Network, **www.gospelcom.net.** This site is an alliance of online Christian ministries from which daily devotions can be read or downloaded into a PDA. (Accessed on September 10, 2002.)

SermonCentral.com, **www.sermoncentral.com**. This site provides the option of searching by keyword, chapter, verse, or topic for more than 30,000 free teaching illustrations and sermons. (Accessed on September 10, 2002.)

StudyLight.org, **www.studylight.org**. This site provides a number of study Bibles that facilitate scriptural comparisons and general study. (Accessed on September 10, 2002.)

Sunday School Resources, **www.kidssundayschool.com**. This site has resources on Sunday school lesson planning, teaching tips, classroom behavior management, and classroom organization. (Accessed on September 10, 2002.)

Talking Bible, **www.talkingbible.com**. This site provides continuous play, chapter by chapter, of the King James version of the New Testament. Real Player is required. It is useful for the visually impaired and for all who wish to hear the Bible read aloud. (Accessed on September 10, 2002.)

SECTION THREE

SUCCEEDING IN A VARIETY OF CHRISTIAN EDUCATION VENUES AND FORMATS

HERE AM I, O LORD!

Where Christian Education Happens

Christians are being called to a new vision of what it means to be a part of the body of Christ, the church in the world.[1]

IN ACCORDANCE WITH THE GREAT COMMISSION (MARK 16:15-18), African American Christians are taught the components of our faith in order to build the kingdom of God and to help us live according to Christ's teachings and expectations for our lives (Matthew 18:18-20). African-centered Christian education, then, is an essential part of personal and congregational life. For individuals, Christian education promotes learning that supports one's personal faith, encourages life changes that enhance our Christian journeys, and that is, in many ways, part of the process by which, after giving our lives, minds, and hearts to Christ, he continues to save us every day. As a kingdom-building tool, African-centered Christian education corrects misinformation, trains minds in the history of the Christian mission and purpose, and creates opportunities for praise and worship with a group of like believers.

African-centered Christian education:

- Provides an educational context that standardizes many of the materials that enhance learning in personal and group formats
- Seeks multiple venues in which Christians can be educated
- Is historically correct: "Some Afrocentric writers claim that all Christian beliefs began in Africa. While Africa was certainly part of the world in which the biblical faith began and developed, as Afrocentric writers have long argued, those who claim that Africa was the cradle of all Christian beliefs overstate the case."[2]
- Supports developing a community of believers equipped to work

toward personal spiritual and mission-driven common goals
- Seeks to engage the congregation in a variety of learning activities to enable Christians to know what they believe and why, and, based on that knowledge, to be effective disciples for Christ

"Christian education, in its simplest form, is educational teaching development designed to transform the life of the Christ-like student or learner. However, as we move forward in this millennium, just as we look at new definitions and new paradigms of learning, development, preaching, and teaching in the faith community, we must also look for the new 'push' and transition in terminology in Christian education. Thus, we have…transitioned our language from that of 'Christian education' to that of 'discipleship.' They [share the same] goal [of building disciples], but [in] our consumer, microwave society, we must stay on the cutting edge of clarity of call, vision, and definition."[3] The shift in the language defining Christian education allows a change in the narrow perceptions that discipleship opportunities are limited to the venues of Bible study and Sunday school.

With disciple making and community building as its primary goals, African-centered Christian education can and must occur in a number of traditional and innovative venues. From traditional programs such as Bible study and Sunday school to those that focus on the specific history, experiences, and needs of African American Christians, many African American churches are viewing Christian education in a more holistic manner, making certain that they use every possible opportunity to provide their members with new information, reinforce established knowledge, address issues that impact the lives of specific groups within the church, and meet targeted congregational learning needs as they arise.

Archival Activities

Church bulletins, newsletters, sick and shut-in lists, curricula for classes and seminars, and other written, audio, or videotaped materials (sermons and transcripts of broadcasts) chronicle the work of the church and inform church members about the focus of ministry, church growth and development, and the achievement of Christian goals, objectives, and activities within the local church.

Arts

African American churches use music, liturgical dance, and drama as parts of worship and to infuse worship and other Christian education venues with reminders of our history and celebration of our culture.

Bible Study

As God's Word, the Bible is an essential tool for Christians. Bible study, provided by the church in formats appropriate for different age groups, and encouraged as a personal activity, is considered a mandatory requirement for dedicated Christians. Departments of Christian education may provide classes that help members learn the history of the Bible, understand the challenges to faith faced by biblical writers, discern the lessons of Christ, and enable guided discussions regarding how to apply Bible teachings to modern life. Participation in small groups gives Bible study a systematic format under the guidance of trained teachers.

TEACHABLE MOMENT

Bible Pledge

This is my Bible.
I am what it says I am.
I can do what it says I can do.
Today I will be taught the Word of God.
I boldly confess my mind is alert, my heart is receptive.
I will never be the same.
I am about to receive the incorruptible, indestructible,
      ever-living seed of the Word of God.
I will never be the same.
Never, never, never.
I will never be the same. In Jesus' name.

Rev. John Osteen, www.lakewood-church.org, see FAQ,
accessed September 10, 2002

Children's Church

Children's church gives young people a chance to worship in an environment designed to meet their learning needs. While the components of worship are unlikely to vary significantly from those of services targeted to adult believers, children's church presents sermons in language more likely to be understood by children and youth and invites active participation through age-appropriate ministries (choir, ushering, and Bible study) that teach the importance of worship.

TEACHABLE MOMENT

I Am the Black Child

I am special, ridicule cannot sway me.
I am strong, obstacles cannot stop me.
I hold my head high, proudly proclaiming my uniqueness.
I hold my pace, continuing forward through adversity.
I am proud of my culture and my heritage.
I am confident that I can achieve my every goal.
I am becoming all that I can be.
I am the black child, I am a child of God.

Mychal Wynn, copyright ©1994

Church School

While church school, usually called Sunday school,[4] is often considered a vehicle for teaching Christian beliefs and values to children, it is also a vibrant educational opportunity for teenagers, adults of all ages, and families. Church school is designed to provide an organizational structure for carrying out the basic teaching ministries of the church. The offerings of church school include Bible study, classes on religious themes (or secular themes viewed through a Christian frame), and fellowship, typically in a small-group setting that encourages the participation of all members. The small-group teaching approach also allows church school to address some of the emotional needs of its congregants—in small groups church members frequently share personal information concerning their conversion and the joys and challenges that attend their Christian journey. Classes are usually divided by age group so that techniques used and materials addressed will be appropriate to age level and developmental stages. Classes for young children, for example, may focus on teaching through memorization of Bible verses and presenting Christian beliefs through Bible stories and question and answer sessions. Adult classes, however, are much more likely to use discussion as a teaching technique so that class members can examine the ways that belief in Christ has changed their lives.

Department of Christian Education

Departments of Christian education are the administrative arm of educational efforts in most churches. Their responsibilities include:
Coordinating and monitoring activities. Coordinating the themes of Christian education programming and related activities among all teaching components (church school, institutes and academies, classes and seminars, and Bible study).
Leadership. Leadership for educational efforts that meet the mission of the local church and advance Christian beliefs and objectives.
Program development. Purchasing, adapting, or designing curriculum materials appropriate to the learning needs of their congregations.
Policymaking. In conjunction with pastoral directives, setting rules and regulations for the development of programs and for the training of Christian education teachers.

Mid-Week Prayer Service

Prayer is essential to the life of the church and prayer service, often called prayer meeting, is where church members can learn and practice the fundamentals of prayer. The early church recognized that prayer was essential to the spiritual life of the individual and the development of a strong corporate community. Understanding that prayer was a tool to help believers become "the light of the world" (Matthew

5:14, John 8:12), and impressed with the prayer life of Jesus, the disciples were moved to ask, "Lord teach us to pray" (Luke 11:1). Prayers offered in the name of Jesus must be consistent with his character, ask only for things he would endorse, occur in harmony with his purpose, and reflect our journey to be as one with Christ.[5] Prayer services, often led by deacons and ministers in training, provide a forum in which church members can be prepared to become a praying people.

TEACHABLE MOMENT

A Black Prayer

Father God
Creator of me
Black in your own image
having breathed into me Your own divine substance
Life
out of that which You are
Love.

Help me to understand Your love and that my destiny—
indeed my salvation is to love You in return with all my heart
soul and mind.

And this love unavoidably must encompass my own Black
self and must include my Black brothers and sisters and the
community we comprise.

Oh God!
Strengthen…prepare…and gird me for the long dark struggle
toward freedom. Help me to live this precious Black life as if
the future and freedom of all Black people depended on me…
alone.

And please God
guide me into those ways that will best utilize the talents
that You have given me in order that I can contribute to the
best of my ability to bringing my people closer…to freedom.
Amen

Vallmer Jordan, Trinity United Church of Christ, Chicago, Illinois

---

New Members Classes

New members classes are provided for persons beginning a relationship with Christ and established Christians who are changing their church membership. For both groups, these classes provide opportunities to:

TEACHABLE MOMENT

Assimilating New Members into Christian Service

When Dr. Cassandra Jones, minister of assimilation at the University Park Baptist Church in Charlotte, North Carolina, discovered that the majority (71 percent) of new members were also new Christians, she viewed this knowledge as a creative challenge. Her title, in fact, reflects the need to assimilate new Christians into the worship and study environment provided by the church, especially since many new members are also the first Christians in several generations of their families. To address these needs for comprehensive Christian training, she and her team designed the Kingdom Citizen's Institute curriculum (KCI), an eight-week process with three-hour class sessions. For each session, reading materials, games, and other related study information are available online. The modules are:

Session 1: Welcome and Overview of the KCI Process. This first session welcomes new members to UPBC and provides them with an overview of the learning journey they will take and of the Christian journey on which they have embarked.

Session 2: Salvation. Participants learn about Christ as the Savior of humanity, the results of man's fall from grace, and the Holy Spirit.

Session 3: Salvation. Participants learn about the challenges that life presents after salvation, Christian precepts (baptism and the Lord's Supper), and Baptist distinctives.

Session 4: Our University Park Baptist Church Family. Class members are shown a welcome videotape (A Walk in the Park) in which the pastor, Rev. Claude Alexander, welcomes them to the church and to a life in the Lord. They are introduced to the church's mission and vision, learn about its ministries (ministry leaders are all invited to give a brief talk on

Learn basic Christian beliefs. New members learn the fundamentals of the salvation process and how to apply Scripture to their daily lives. **Discuss the requirements of discipleship.** New members explore the discipline required to be disciples of Christ. Classes often teach the importance of prayer, fasting, Bible study, ministry participation, and worship.

---

the work of their ministries), are instructed in church etiquette, and are given a "grand tour" of the UPBC, a process that helps them see ministry in action and teaches them the history of the new church building.

Session 5: PLACE (Personality Blends, Learning Spiritual Gifts, Abilities, Connecting Passion to Ministry, and Experiences in Life). Understanding that effective ministry requires passion, the KCI asks new members to identify the things they love to do, rather than identifying the ministry they want to work with. They receive guidance for determining how their passion matches ministry needs, then make a covenant pledge for ministry participation.

Session 6: Every Member an Intercessor (A Lifestyle Prayer) and Every Member a Witness (Sharing Your Faith). This session is designed to teach new members the importance of prayer on behalf of others and the church's dedication to the Great Commission.

Session 7: Every Member a Steward (Faith, Family, Fellowship, Finances, and Fitness). This session teaches that stewardship, including maintaining fitness and health, are essential requirements of Christianity.

Session 8: GRADUATION CLASS! This class is a celebration in which class members do evaluations of the class and discuss the process, sign up to two ministry declaration cards over which a covenant prayer is prayed, contribute to a church debt reducing offering, and receive instructions for full church membership. On the fourth Sunday of each month at the 10:30 a.m. service, the graduates are announced—their names are read and their ministries are announced to cheers of support. After service they take a picture with the pastor and are honored with a dinner to which their friends and family members are invited.

Information from e-mail, fax, and telephone interviews
in August and September 2002

Learn the history and organization of their local church. Learning church heritage provides members with a sense of their church's rich traditions.

Learn the pastoral vision for church growth and development. Use this class to inform new members of church plans.

Make Christian education a positive experience. Too often Christian educators get caught up in teaching the "should nots" rather than the "shoulds" and in recounting sins rather than discussing the salvation we receive when we give our lives to Christ and work together to build his church. While the church must teach what Christ expects of us, Christian educators must also create an accepting environment that encourages new members to remain involved with their new congregation and that teaches, through example, that God is love.

TEACHABLE MOMENT

Moving from Pain to Empowerment

Black congregations can ill-afford to mirror the oppressions they received from the dominant culture. Recognizing the value of communal interdependence is the first step toward bringing together the dual experience of being saved by hope and being empowered to serve. The most obvious expression of this value is when new members are oriented into the life of the congregation. Providing information about ministry meetings, prayer services, Bible classes, and other activities is an excellent way to invite new member involvement. But the real connecting and sustaining power comes through involvement as ministry partners. Think about your ministry and how the "cliques" within it may mirror the same kind of rejection that the African slaves experienced in the white church. Now imagine the level of spiritual power available to us as a community of faith if we step out on the promise of God's saving grace, armed with the uniting and welcoming perspective of our ancestors.

Dr. Julia Speller, "Retreat Manual for 2002: Saved By Hope, Empowered to Serve." Trinity United Church of Christ

Ask questions. Because members join the church at different points in their Christian journey, classes should explore membership, Christian responsibilities, and the joys of building a relationship with Christ.

Preaching

Preachers are also Christian educators. "The black preacher is integral to the nurture of the spiritual life of the black church. The preacher is often pastor, community leader, prophet, civil rights advocate, and the chief administrator of the community's most independent enterprise, the black church."[6] All of these pastoral roles provide opportunities for Christian education. However, because the majority of church members attend worship services only, sermons (and observations of preachers in other public venues) are the primary manner in which many worshipers learn theology. "Educational centers and programs are in operation by African American churches and institutions across this nation but…the majority of…these communities get their theology from the preached Word rather than through the various Christian education ministries."[7]

Programs for Targeted Populations

Christian education also provides for the spiritual needs of specific groups within the church.

Men's groups. These groups may help men address their roles as husbands and fathers who are committed to Christ, and facilitate discussion of the particular challenges faced by African American men.[8]

Singles ministries. To help single people resist the temptations of the secular world to build relationships casually built on carnal desires, singles ministries teach the responsibilities of building Christian relationships and provide opportunities for singles to meet and marry people with similar religious beliefs.

Special needs populations. Increasingly, churches provide Christian education services for people with special needs. Many churches, for example, provide interpretation services that allow deaf members to be fully involved in classes and worship. (Christian education for individuals with special needs is addressed in more detail in Chapter Nine.)

Women's groups. Christian education targeted to women whose lives and roles are informed by their Christian beliefs provides them with an opportunity to deepen their personal commitment to Christ through their personal lives and relationships built within their families.

Youth Programs. Youth programs teach Christian beliefs and the expectations of discipleship in a way that is appropriate to the needs and developmental levels of children and teenagers. (Youth programs are also discussed in their own section in this chapter.)

Special Programs in Christian Education

Academies and Institutes

Many African American churches offer academy or institute programs that focus on a specific theme for the year, or a consistent theme over time. For example, the H. Beecher Hicks Sr. Institute of Great Preaching at Metropolitan Baptist Church in Washington, D.C., presents well-regarded preachers from churches of various denominations and congregational sizes who share their perspectives on the annual theme based on biblical teachings, personal experiences, issues facing the African American community, and concerns and needs of the congregation. All are masters of **homiletics** and provide spirited preaching that enriches the life of the church.

Academies sponsored by churches also structure Bible study, theological studies, discipleship strategies, and ministry opportunities for members. Some churches provide classes (alone or in conjunction with local colleges and universities) that lead to certificates of study, while others have accredited educational academies that grant credits toward degrees. (See the Teachable Moment on page 133.)

Lecture Series

Lecture series are often week-long events held by churches to address a theme important to the life of the church. For example, a lecture series may have a week of lectures on the importance of tithing in an effort to assist church members with responsible stewardship. Lecture series may also teach church members through detailed explanations of the historical and current meanings of a particular passage of Scripture or an event in the life of Jesus.

TEACHABLE MOMENT

Becoming Disciples through Bible Study
Mississippi Boulevard Christian Church, Memphis, Tennessee

This four-year training program provides Christians with a disciplined course of study each September through May and has graduated more than five hundred students since its inception in 1997. Each of its four components takes one year to complete:

Disciple I. This foundation course provides the structure and discipline for comprehensive Bible study and serves as a prerequisite for the other classes in the *Becoming Disciples through Bible Study* series. This course begins with the story of Creation, challenging disciples to submit themselves personally to "examination by Scripture" and to be changed by God's Word.

Disciple II. In the second course, "Into the Word, Into the World," disciples are taught advanced Bible study skills, encouraged in the practice of spiritual discipline, provided reinforcement for the importance of Bible study to witness and service in the world, and learn about the transforming power of Scripture.

Disciple III. The third module, "Remember Who You Are," focuses on confronting the "persistent questions of the prophets and Paul," namely, What are the priorities in your life? and What are the priorities in society? Looking at the world through a scriptural lens, disciples learn to apply their answers to their lives within the supportive structure of their church community.

Disciple IV. The final year of the course, "Under the Tree of Life," concentrates on the biblical Writings such as Psalms, Proverbs, and Ecclesiastes, which focus on "living toward completion." The course also discusses the climax of the gospel message and describes the promise of the gospel as pictured in the book of Revelation.

Rev. Nadine Burton, Associate Minister for Christian Education, Mississippi Boulevard Christian Church, e-mail and fax interviews, September 17–19, 2002

Retreats

Time away from everyday life frequently allows church members to regain a directed focus on issues related to faith, church growth and development, and leadership directions. Retreats typically follow an agenda that provides an outline of expected learning goals and outcomes. Church members are then expected to implement what they have learned in their personal lives and in the activities of the church.

Revivals

Christians strive to be Christ-like but fail. Revivals, **evangelistic** efforts that bring new souls to Christ, are designed to refresh our spirits and renew our faith through preaching missions. They often occur in the spring, at a time when nature, too, renews itself.

Seminars

Christian seminars address issues that help Christians maintain a determined walk with Christ. They often deal with contemporary issues such as strengthening marriages, managing finances, and raising children. Seminars may also approach a Christian theme over a period of weeks or months, allowing participants the luxury of prolonged learning and reflection.

Workshops

Workshops provide an intensive teaching moment that usually lasts for a day or a weekend. During the workshops, church members meet to address a theme that is important to their journey towards effective discipleship.

Vacation Bible School

Whether conducted as a day program or a sleep-away camp, Vacation Bible School is a program oriented to meet the learning needs of children and young teenagers. It serves as a continuation of church school through a different, fun, and activity-filled environment during the summer months.

Worship

Worship "is defined as the celebrative response to what God has done, is doing, and promises to do."[9] It is an event that happens on a weekly basis in most churches, usually on Sunday mornings. Although local churches host a variety of activities, programs, and congregational experiences, worship is what most people think of when they use the word "church." Because of the community perception of its importance, it is also the place where most church members, longtime visitors, and occasional worshipers are likely to receive information about Christian beliefs, the components of faith, the mission of the church, church activities, and the importance of church ministries to personal development and church growth. According to Robert E. Webber, author of *Worship Is a Verb*, there are eight principles of worship, principles that the author of this book views as also true of worship as an educational activity in the church:

- Worship celebrates Christ
- Worship tells and acts out the Christ-events
- In worship God speaks and acts
- Worship is an act of communication
- In worship we respond to God and each other
- Return worship to the people
- All creation joins in worship
- Worship as a way of life[10]

These principles teach that worship is an active and interactive process that provides information and participatory experiences, is a sanctuary where the Spirit of God resides, and is centered on a community of believers involved in activities that demonstrate a belief in, a commitment to, and an adoration of Christ. In worship services parishioners:

Learn theology. Christian beliefs are shared through pastoral teaching, the singing of hymns, and the reading of the Bible as regular parts of worship service. Hymns, for example, "communicate to others what we are about and what we believe. They also communicate an affirmation of the divine and how we experience God in our lives and spiritual journey. Hymns take on the form of a dialogue within the community of worshipers as well as in our individual devotions and prayers to God."[11]

Observe Christian holy days. Though most African American denominations do not follow a **liturgical year,**[12] they observe a Christian calendar year that includes special services for Christmas and Holy Week (Palm Sunday, Good Friday, and Easter, which is also called Resurrection Sunday in some churches). By participating in these celebrations and ceremonies, worshipers learn their importance to the faith and become part of a community of believers gathered to commemorate important moments in the life of Christ.

Observe the importance of church rituals. A lot can be learned by paying attention to the rituals engaged in by the local church. Church **ordinances** such as baptism and the Lord's Supper, infant blessings, and celebration of events special to the life of the church (Mother's Day, Father's Day, and church, pastoral, and choir anniversaries, for example), and observance of moments important to its members all provide a focus on what the church values and honors.

Participate in and learn the order of worship. Worship often occurs in a manner that is repeated weekly, providing an additional ritual of the church. "The order of worship varies among [African American] churches but often follows a basic format. However, they all tend to include devotion, a call to worship, prayer, Scripture reading, congregational singing, songs by the choir, an offering, a sermon, and a time when 'the doors of the church are opened' to welcome new souls to Christ."[13]

Learn the role of church leaders. The pastor, deacons and elders, church officers (such as the church clerk), presidents of church ministries, and other lay leaders have responsibilities that are carried out in worship services. Worshipers learn the roles of church leaders in the structure of their local church by observing their activities within the worship context.

Understand the contribution of church ministries to the Christian community. Many ministries are involved in worship. For example, the music ministry acts in the capacity of worship leader, guiding the congregation in worship through song. Ushers, the gatekeepers of the church, assure that order is maintained during the worship service and are often assigned to collect the offering. By assisting the pastor in distributing the Lord's Supper to the congregation, deacons contribute their leadership to a sacred rite of the African American church.

TEACHABLE MOMENT

Worship as a Strategy for Survival

[African Americans] grew as a result of intense worship. Our faith made us strong and we were able to endure a lot more than people are enduring today, all because of our worship. We looked at the world and knew right away that the "other world" was really our home.... Success in society was always linked to our involvement in the African American church context and, for many of us, it was the first place that we were allowed to speak publicly (Christmas pageants, Easter plays, Vacation Bible School programs).

Toney L. McNair. *Let's Have Church! A Guide for Worship in the African American Context.* Norfolk, Virginia: Greater Harvest and Worship Ministries (757-622-4458), 2001, page 6

Youth Programs

Targeted to meeting the Christian education needs of teenagers and young adults, youth programs provide Bible study and classes that present Christian beliefs and values and address the issues of identity, sexuality, relationships, familial responsibilities, and future planning that are essential to youth development.

Notes

1. *Michael W. Foss.* Power Surge: Six Marks of Discipleship for a Changing Church. *Minneapolis: Fortress Press, 2000, page 8.*

2. *Craig S. Keener and Glenn Usry.* Defending Black Faith: Answers to Tough Questions About African-American Christianity. *Downers Grove, Illinois: Intervarsity Press, 1997, page 42.*

3. *Rev. Barbara Peacock, Minister of Discipleship, University Park Baptist Church, Charlotte, North Carolina, e-mail interview, August 28, 2002.*

4. *Many churches are now providing church school on other days of the week, frequently Saturdays.*

5. *Dr. Harry Blake.* Seminar X: Revitalizing Mid-Week Bible Study and Prayer Meeting. *Minister's Division of the National Baptist Congress of Christian*

Education. St. Louis, Missouri, June 17–21, 2002, pages 187–195.

6. The African American Experience in Holy Bible: The African American Jubilee Edition. *New York: American Bible Society, 1999, page 27.*

7. *Olin P. Moyd.* The Sacred Art: Preaching and Theology in the African American Tradition. *Valley Forge: Judson Press, 1995, page 9.*

8. *The specific Christian teachings about male and female roles will differ greatly among African American churches based on their interpretation of Scripture.*

9. *Toney L. McNair.* Let's Have Church! A Guide for Worship in the African American Context. *Norfolk, Virginia: Greater Harvest and Worship Ministries (757-622-4458), 2001, page 5.*

10. *Robert E. Webber.* Worship Is a Verb. *Peabody, Massachusetts: Hendrickson Publishers, Inc., 1995, page 13.*

11. *James Abbington.* Let Mt. Zion Rejoice! Music in the African American Church. *Valley Forge: Judson Press, 2001, page 57.*

12. *Abbington.* Let Mt. Zion Rejoice! *page 73.*

13. *Lora-Ellen McKinney.* Total Praise: An Orientation to Black Baptist Belief and Worship. *Valley Forge: Judson Press, 2003, pages 38–39.*

WHAT SHALL I RENDER?

Choosing Christian Education Materials
that Meet Congregational Needs

New generations bring new expectations.[1]

ALL CHURCHES NEED CHRISTIAN EDUCATION AND HAVE RECEIVED A scriptural mandate to provide it to their members (Mark 16:15, Matthew 6:33). However, churches differ greatly in the ways that Christian education might best be presented to their congregations. To determine the most appropriate materials for Christian education, Christian educators must be aware of the:

Adaptability of their congregation to change. Change is a common human difficulty. Many churches have used certain definitions of Christian education for many years or have limited their teaching materials to those of a specific vendor. While most church members won't protest the use of new Christian education strategies, educators should expect some resistance to programs that differ greatly from the norm.

Basic educational level of their congregations. Materials may need to be selected or designed based on the congregation's reading level.

Congregational age groupings. Church members require materials appropriate to their age and developmental levels.

Desires of congregants for Christian education. Church members seek knowledge. Some desire basic information that is presented in traditional Christian education formats—Christian beliefs, denominational history, and history of the Old and New Testaments—while others wish to learn how to conduct themselves as Christian singles, married couples, and parents, or how to be good stewards of the resources provided for them by God. Congregational wishes for different types of Christian education content may broaden the definition of Christian education used by a local church, provide educators with new ideas about meaningful Christian education, and inform the design of classes that assist the Christian walk of church members.

By understanding their congregations (adaptability to change, basic educational levels, congregational age groupings, desires for certain forms of or content in Christian education, and perceptions of themselves as Christians) Christian educators are better prepared to provide formats, materials, and teacher training that meet congregational needs.

TEACHABLE MOMENT

When I Say I Am a Christian

When I say… "I am a Christian" I'm not shouting "I am saved." I'm whispering "I was lost." That's why I chose this way.

When I say… "I am a Christian" I don't speak of this with pride. I'm confessing that I stumble and need someone to be my guide.

When I say… "I am a Christian" I'm not trying to be strong. I'm professing that I'm weak and pray for strength to carry on.

When I say… "I am a Christian" I'm not bragging of success. I'm admitting I have failed and cannot ever pay the debt.

When I say… "I am a Christian" I'm not claiming to be perfect. My flaws are too visible, but God believes I am worth it.

When I say… "I am a Christian" I still feel the sting of pain. I have my share of heartaches which is why I speak His name.

When I say… "I am a Christian" I do not wish to judge. I have no authority. I only know I'm loved.

Author unknown

Curriculum Decisions

Every department of Christian education has important decisions to determine what materials best meet the needs of their congregation: **What is the definition of Christian education used in the church?** Does the pastor or the church view Christian education as Sunday school only, Sunday school and Bible study primarily, or encourage a broad-based holistic definition of Christian education? (See Chapter One for definitions of Christian education provided by prominent Christian educators, authors, and local churches from around the country.)

Who comprises the congregation? A congregation of mostly new Christians may benefit from a different kind of curriculum, program, or approach than a congregation that has a mixture of new Christians, new members who are established Christians, and established Christians who have been church members for a period of time.

What is the budget for Christian education? Making Christian education a priority requires having a budget for it that is sufficient to its needs.

What resources are available? In addition to money to purchase, adapt, or design materials for Christian education, Christian education departments must be aware of the resources that can help them implement effective programs that meet biblical requirements, denominational wishes, pastoral directives, and congregational needs. Those resources will include materials available from bookstores, catalogs, websites, local colleges, seminaries, and universities, local and regional experts who can serve as consultants, and members of the congregation.

Curriculum decisions will most often focus on three categories of materials that are readily available to Christian education program directors, Sunday school superintendents, and Christian educators responsible for specific classes, workshops, seminars, or programs:

- Purchased Christian education materials. Nicely designed workbooks, quarterly or annual teaching modules, and denominationally approved materials are available for purchase from Christian education businesses and church groups.

- Adapted Christian education materials. Materials purchased from Christian education businesses may meet many but not all of the needs of an individual church. Departments of Christian education may find it appropriate to supplement purchased materials with additional information or activities, or to eliminate from those materials modules or chapters that they find inconsistent with their interpretation of Christian beliefs or the Christian practice of their congregation. (While it is often necessary to adapt materials to meet church needs, this author encourages Christian educators to consider presenting controversial information for discussion, particularly for teen and adult learners. Class participants face material inconsistent with their beliefs on a daily basis and can be greatly aided by having opportunities to discuss them and address the manner in which they are or are not supported by what they have learned about the Word of God.)

• Designed Christian education materials. No matter whether a church is large or small, in its membership are likely to be those involved with or interested in education, as well as those capable of researching the needs of the congregation for Christian education and designing materials that best meet their developmental and discipleship needs.

Purchasing African-Centered Christian Education Materials

Departments of Christian education have excellent options for building their curricula from materials purchased from a variety of sources. The benefit of buying materials from established organizations and companies is that they work to present lessons consistent with Christian theology, design materials with an understanding of developmental learning styles, and provide an array of support materials (youth games, classroom displays, student workbooks, and teacher manuals).

Many prepared materials are designed specifically for Sunday school and are organized to provide weekly lessons for age groups from child to adult, aided by materials for teacher training at each age level. A number of groups that prepare Sunday school materials also provide curricula for Bible study and Vacation Bible School.

Materials for classes, seminars, and workshops are also available for purchase, though they may require more research on the part of Christian education departments or individual teachers. Most Christian education materials, curricula and books, are available for purchase through regularly distributed catalogs, web searches, online bookstores, denominational conventions, and religious bookstores.

The following are categories of Christian education materials available to local churches:

Africentric materials. Christian education materials dedicated to the needs of African American Christians are readily available from several sources.

- African American denominations. The conventions of AME, AME Zion, Baptists, COGIC, Disciples of Christ, and United Churches of Christ churches provide access to Christian education materials through their annual meetings, denominational convocations of Christian educators, and websites. (See reference lists at the end of each section for the websites of African American denominations.)

- Homeland Ministries. This group of the Disciples of Christ hosts leadership conferences, designs teaching materials, distributes the African American Faith and Life newsletter, and provides technical assistance and curriculum development support through AACEN, the African American Christian Education Network (888-DHM-2631, www.homelandministries.org).

- Urban Ministries, Inc. Urban Ministries, Inc. considers itself to be the largest independently owned and operated religious publishing company in the United States. Its mission states that the organization is "called of God to create, produce, and distribute quality Christian educational products; and to provide quality Christian education training which will empower God's people, especially within the African American community, to evangelize, disciple, and prepare persons to serve Jesus Christ, his Kingdom, and Church."[2] UMI provides books and videos, and materials for Sunday school, Vacation Bible School, and the study of black history (www.urbanministries.com).

- Bibles. The African American Jubilee Edition Bible provides supplementary materials that allow African American Christians to read the Bible through their cultural lens (see Section One resources).

- Geographically correct maps. Maps that present countries in proper geographical proportion can be purchased (along with teaching materials). A Peters Projection map (www.google.com, keyword: Peters Projection Map or 800-736-1293) or those located with study guides in the back of the African American Jubilee Edition Bible (see Section One resources) are good choices.

- Websites dedicated to African American history. Christian educators may find information helpful to designing Africentric materials or adapting other materials to meet the needs of African American congregations on www.google.com (keywords: recommended African American websites).[3]

Denominational materials. Christian denominations (Africentric and non-ethnic) frequently design educational materials, based on their interpretation of Scripture and the specific beliefs of their denomination, that are available for purchase by their affiliated churches. These materials are typically structured to provide weekly lessons for Sunday school programs. For example, the American Baptist and Methodist churches make learning materials available through their respective catalogs, conventions, and online bookstores (www.abc-usa.org and www.umc.org).

General resources. Christian education materials can be found in a number of easily accessible places:

- religious bookstores sponsored by individual churches
- religious bookstores located in most major cities (see "Books" or "Bookstores, Religious" in the Yellow Pages)
- secular bookstores with large sections on religion (for example, Barnes and Noble or Borders Books)
- local college and university libraries, World Wide Web search engine investigations (www.google.com is an excellent search engine that eliminates a lot of online clutter—use keywords "Christian education," "African American Christian education," "Sunday school," Vacation Bible School")
- reference lists (such as those provided at the end of each section of this book)
- online bookstores (www.amazon.com, www.borders.com, and www.barnesandnoble.com)
- websites that promote Scripture lessons and lesson plans

The potential downside to buying purchased materials is that they are designed to meet the needs of a broad array of Christian learners and may not address the specific needs of a particular congregation. Departments of Christian education may choose to adapt materials to better meet congregational needs or may choose to design their own curriculum and related materials.

Adapting Christian Education Materials

Directors of Christian education, Sunday school superintendents, and Christian educators may wish to adjust materials they have purchased or that are in their files. Materials available for purchase should provide appropriate religious content and an organization and structure that facilitate teaching and learning. Despite their usefulness for a specific congregation or denomination, African American Christian educators often need to adapt materials to increase their appropriateness for use with certain age groups, to improve information available on specific topics, to enhance the manner in which theological issues are addressed as they relate to African Americans, or to update materials. Considerations for adapting materials include:

Inappropriateness of available materials. Congregations may need materials for non-English speaking congregations or learners with special needs. Christian educators may also wish to eliminate or add certain issues not addressed in their course materials.

Wishing to teach topics not addressed by available materials. While addressing educational needs from a Christian perspective, most professionally designed materials aim for the middle of the road. This ensures maximum sales to the largest number of churches. To make certain that their teaching includes issues important to the beliefs of their local church or denomination, or that are in line with the recommendations of regional or national Christian organizations, conventions, or assemblies with which a specific church affiliates, Christian educators often add vital sources of information.

Financial constraints. When the Christian education budget is limited or the purchase of new materials is not possible for other reasons, Christian educators may wish to evaluate available materials and add to them in ways that create interest for learners.

Designing Materials for Your Congregation

Many African American Christian educators find that their best option is to design their own materials. They know their congregations better than anyone else and may be best suited to designing curricula for use in their churches. Those who wish to do so should:

Survey the congregation. While it is clear that the congregation will require certain information on theology, stewardship, church history, and other traditional forms of Christian education, it is important to learn from members some basic data to help Christian educators determine the content and format of courses, when they should be offered, and the persons who are likely to attend them. Surveys, distributed in paper form or online, should ask members the following data and use the results to design programs: demographic information (age, gender, years of experience with Christian education, years of church membership, marital status, number and ages of children, educational level); how often they attend services and classes; ministries in which they are involved; the type of work they do; hours and days that they can attend classes; whether and how their grandparents and parents were involved in a local church; and what they are most interested in learning.

Create a curriculum committee. Identify congregants who are educators and those who have skills in the areas important to African-centered curriculum development (e.g., African-centered biblical knowledge, ministry development, technology use, stages of child and adult development, the arts) and develop a committee that, based on survey findings, can write a curriculum that meets congregational needs.

TEACHABLE MOMENT

University Park Baptist Church
Charlotte, North Carolina

Understanding that Christian educators come to their vocation with different amounts of formal training in teaching, the department of Christian education at the University Park Baptist Church has developed a curriculum for teaching educators how to conduct classes for students of different ages and who are in different phases of their relationships with Christ. This curriculum was written under the direction of the director of Christian education with a team of educational experts from the congregation.

Coordinate curriculum ideas with church mission and plans. Many churches operate according to strategic plans. Curriculum ideas must match the mission of the local church, fit into budgetary considerations for each year, and be in line with long-term plans determined by church leadership.

Create a work plan and process. Assign tasks based on a realistic schedule, meet established deadlines, strive for excellence, and implement Christian education plans that will meet congregational wishes and needs for personal growth and development.

Teach church history. To enhance the appreciation for the place in which they worship and serve, it is essential that congregants learn the history of their denomination and of their particular church—its founding, its ministers past and present, its mission and vision, and its history of community contributions.

TEACHABLE MOMENT

Church History
First AME Church, Los Angeles

In 1787, the African Methodist Episcopal Church was founded by God under the inspired tenacity of Bishop Richard Allen. Allen taught himself to read and worked to pay for his and his family's freedom from slavery.

The First AME Church of Los Angeles was founded in 1872 by Biddy Mason, a woman who walked behind a Mormon wagon train. In her seven-month journey from Mississippi to Salt Lake City to San Bernadino, California, she walked thousands of miles, herding cattle and tending to her three daughters.

Rev. Joyce Randall, Director of Christian Education, First AME,
e-mail interview, August 28–30, 2002

Improving Christian Education through Technology

The appropriate use of technology increases the capacity of Christian educators to be effective in their work in the following ways:

Administration

- Online course registration. Church websites can be designed to provide an online registration option for those who wish to enroll in Christian education courses. This provides for departments of Christian education an accurate database of classes offered, persons enrolled, and class schedules.
- E-mail registration verification. Registrants can receive a confirmation of their class registration via e-mail. While this can be done manually (someone sends an e-mail confirmation to each registrant), systems can also be designed to do this automatically.
- Resource management. In the event that a class appears to have too few registrants, e-mail notices can be sent to those who had registered, providing them with alternative classes.
- Statistics. Websites can keep statistics on the numbers of people who log on for specific information and can be used to get their assessment of the usefulness of the information received.

Community Outreach

- Online Bible study. Many churches provide Bible study on their websites. This offering can duplicate the content of weekly Bible study conducted at the church or can be an independent offering. Churches without the resources to design their own Bible study can have their website linked to an existing Bible study service such as the daily Bible reading available on www.beliefnet.com.
- Online church school. Many churches use denominational materials for Sunday or other church school classes. These lessons or those adapted or designed by a local church can be posted to their websites to encourage independent study and to provide the lessons for those who cannot attend church school classes.
- Evaluation of online classes. As part of the statistics kept by the website, churches can post and tally evaluation forms for online Christian education classes.

Teaching Assistance

- Computer learning games. Many Christian websites have stores through which child appropriate Bible-based computers games can be purchased.

- Visual aids. Use PowerPoint, overheads, and large print documents to aid visual learners and those with aging eyes.

Worship

- Closed captioning. Churches with large screens in the sanctuary can provide closed captioning services for the deaf and hard of hearing (check with local television stations about how to purchase the necessary technology), or use a split screen for sign language interpreters.
- Streaming video sermons. Sermons can be placed on websites in real or delayed time and are accessible to those who have sound cards and video viewing capabilities on their computers. Churches without the required video capacity can provide audio sermons online as well. This makes sermons available to the sick and shut in and traveling members and is an opportunity for further study for those able to attend services.
- Large screen or video announcements. To decrease paper costs and waste and to streamline services, announcements can be posted on video screens around the church or presented on a sanctuary screen.

TEACHABLE MOMENT

We learn and grow together
And share the Living Word
Our hopes and dreams are realized
By teaching what we've heard.

25th Anniversary Song of the Association of Christian Education, United Church of Christ, www.ctconfucc.org, accessed on September 10, 2002

Notes

1. *Lyle E. Schaller. What Have We Learned? Lessons for the Church in the 21st Century. Nashville: Abingdon Press, 2001, page 19.*

2. *www.urbanministries.com*

3. *Use quotations around the keywords for best search results.*

Top Ten Tips for Succeeding in Many Christian Education Venues and Formats

1. View Christian education broadly.

2. Know your congregation.[1]

3. Establish goals for Christian education.

4. Assess congregational needs for specific Christian education topics.

5. Develop a curriculum committee.

6. Create a work plan and defined timeline.

7. Assign and monitor responsibilities based on Christian education goals and work plan requirements.

8. Make curriculum decisions based on church definition of Christian education, congregational needs, and human and financial resources.

9. Purchase, adapt, or design curriculum materials that fit your Christian educational goals.

10. Use technology to enhance the administration and provision of Christian education.[2]

Notes

1. To effectively provide Christian education it is essential to know who is in your congregation (ages, socio-economic status, professions, proximity to the church) and their needs (new members or new to the faith, established members, populations requiring specific considerations or accommodations).

2. Technology might scare you, but it is a necessary tool and someone in the congregation is expert at using technology to teach. Find them, learn from them, and use them effectively.

Preparation for the Journey

1. What is the definition of Christian education in my church?

2. Is our program of Christian education related to our African-ness?

3. What members of our congregation have skills and interests that would enhance our program of Christian education?

4. What members of our congregation have the skills and interests to be effective members of the Christian Education Curriculum Committee?

5. What Christian education issues are of interest to the congregation?

6. Does our Christian education budget meet our operational needs?

7. What forms of technology will improve our ability to provide Christian education for all of our members?

REFERENCES

FOR PROVIDING CHRISTIAN EDUCATION IN A VARIETY OF SETTINGS AND FOR SPECIFIC GROUPS

Kenneth D. Blazier and Linda R. Isham, editors. *The Teaching Church at Work: A Manual for a Board of Christian Education.* Valley Forge: Judson Press, 1994. This book is designed as a practical tool for those who are developing, reorganizing, or improving new or existing Christian education departments.

Floyd M. Massey and Samuel B. McKinney. *Church Administration in the Black Perspective.* Valley Forge: Judson Press, 1979. Considered a seminal text on black church administration, this book, originally published in 1976, has been consistently updated to provide current guidelines for church administration. "The text also explores how the African heritage and slave experience have molded traditions that are significant in black church life today."

Toney L. McNair. *Let's Have Church! A Guide for Worship in the African American Context.* Norfolk, Virginia: Greater Harvest and Worship Ministries (757-622-4458), 2001. Defining worship as a celebration of God's promises to us, this workbook discusses the importance of personal devotion to God, the traditions and characteristics of African American worship, and helpful recommendations for rethinking the worship moment.

Church School

LaVerne Tolbert. *Teaching Like Jesus.* Grand Rapids, Michigan: Zondervan Publishing House, 2001. This book is designed to make the Gospels relevant to today's church members. Using a four-step device for teaching the examples set by Christ's teachings in the Gospels (Hook, Book, Look, Took), this practical guide provides innovative teaching strategies for church schools in the urban, suburban, or rural local church.

Programs for Targeted Groups

Josh McDowell and Bob Hostetler, editors. *One Year Book of Youth Devotions.* Carol Stream, Illinois: Tyndale House Publishers, 1999. This book is designed to help youth apply Scripture to the problems they confront in daily life.

Sharon Daloz Parks. *Big Questions, Worthy Dreams: Mentoring Young Adults in Their Search for Meaning, Purpose, and Faith.* New York: Jossey-Bass, 2000. Parks uses psychological theory to provide strategies for helping young people set priorities to center their lives through a determined focus on faith and spirituality.

BUILDING A SUCCESSFUL AFRICAN-CENTERED CHRISTIAN EDUCATION PROGRAM

CHAPTER TWELVE

ON A JOURNEY TOWARD JESUS

Building Success into Christian Education Programs

I believe the time has come for every congregation to set its priorities on the basis of what God is calling it to do and to meet the needs of people.[1]

CHRISTIAN EDUCATION IS SUCCESSFUL WHEN WE SET PRIORITIES THAT allow us to address God's mission for the Church in the context of our local congregational needs. In essence, the task of Christian education is "to equip each church member to more effectively perform his [or her] God-given assignment in the body of Christ."[2] Learning our roles within the body of Christ requires an increased understanding of the Word of God, the ability to identify our spiritual gifts, and the capacity to meet our faith-related learning needs within a community of like believers.

Christian education in the African American context seeks to expand discipleship through a connection with our African past. "Africans in their act of worship live close to the land. Prayers to God relate directly to rain, fertility, and the welfare of humans, cattle, and fields…. God is the one who makes the sun rise and set, the mountains quake, and the rivers overflow. He heals the sick, helps the barren, and aids those in distress."[3]

Africentric Christianity also connects us with our African American history, understanding its complexity and its capacity to meet many of our needs. "At its inception, the black church has been the most important and dominant institution in African American communities. The black church carries burdens and performs roles and functions beyond the boundaries of spiritual nurturing in politics, economics, education, music, and culture. It has been involved in the missions that embrace domestic activities such as family, education, urban ministries, and the institutional church, to name a few."[4]

The need for these joint histories to be effectively communicated to our members requires us to identify within our churches all possible venues for Christian education. While it is important that the traditional formats for Christian education reflect our dedication to excellence, many successful programs of Christian education move beyond worship service, Sunday school, and mid-week Bible study to incorporate classes and activities that prepare African American Christians for the daily conduct of their lives and that create opportunities for developing strong and supportive communities of faith. Success in Africentric Christian education programs results from our intentional efforts to:

- Teach our Afri-Christian history
- Restore African-centered values into Christian education efforts
- Coordinate Christian education with the church's mission
- Set attainable goals and establish work plans
- Create a learning congregation
- Recruit, train, and retain Christian educators
- Market Christian education programs inside the church and in the outside community

Coordinate Christian Education with the Mission of the Church

Departments of Christian education serve as the coordinating arm of educational efforts in the local church. Christian education is much more than courses designed to meet learning needs. Educational offerings within the church must meet two church missions—the mission that Christ has given us to develop the Church of God by fulfilling the Great Commission and the mission of each local church to meet those objectives in the manner appropriate for them.

The mission of the local church identifies the manner in which the church interprets its theological prerogatives and empowers its congregation to interact within the church family and in the community.

Because church missions are not always readily evident, Christian educators can ensure that members understand how their church seeks to expand the kingdom of God by:

Posting the mission in places where it will be seen by all church members. The church mission can be placed on centrally located plaques, in the church bulletin, and on the church website.

Discussing the church mission in Christian education courses and venues. Course offerings that discuss the church mission in the context of the history of the local church and its work can teach church members about how God has moved in their congregation over the years.

Requiring participants to learn the mission. Child-focused courses and new members classes can require that participants memorize the church mission as part of their entry into informed church membership.

TEACHABLE MOMENT

Church Mission

First AME Church exists to embody Christ both WITHIN THE WALLS and BEYOND THE WALLS by equipping all people regardless of race or origin—spiritually, economically, politically, and morally—making the Word become flesh through tools in education, health, housing, feeding, job procurement, business and incubator loans, venture capital, transportation, adoptions, mentoring, and other ministries of outreach.

First AME Church, Los Angeles, California

The mission of the Metropolitan Baptist Church ministries is to bring persons into a saving and redemptive relationship as Disciples of Jesus Christ. We are a Spiritual body whose only foundation is the Word of God. We fulfill our ministry as we proclaim and teach, pray and worship, forgive and reconcile. As we live by Christ's example, we empower others to carry out the commands of God. We seek only to be God's servants as agents of healing and wholeness in a wounded and fragmented world.

Metropolitan Baptist Church, Washington, D.C.

Departments of Christian education effectively coordinate their efforts with church missions by matching each Christian education goal to the stated mission of the church. The church mission identifies the overall goal to which Christian education should aspire. For example, as noted in the previous Teachable Moment, the mission of First AME Church of Los Angeles clearly values educational efforts dedicated to inreach and outreach that are attuned to addressing social issues that impact African Americans. Metropolitan Baptist Church of Washington, D.C., focuses on relational ministries that bring souls to Christ for the purpose of salvation. While these two churches have the same theological and social aims, their Christian education programs could, in fact, reflect different emphases based on the priorities stated in their missions.

Set Goals and Establish Work Plans

No program of Christian education can succeed unless it is coordinated with the mission of the church, focused on meeting a set of defined goals, and conducted according to a carefully designed plan. Essential to meeting the specific learning needs of the church membership, Christian education goals must be measurable and in alignment with its purpose as defined by church leadership. Christian educators must prepare themselves to design programatic excellence. Planning processes for Christian education departments should:

Assess what exists. Determine the status of the current program. Is it meeting needs? Does it require expansion or is it smart to focus on fewer offerings? What is the level of participant satisfaction? What are the pastor's perceptions about the success of the Christian education department?

Define an organizational structure. Who will be in the department or on the board? What are the job descriptions and the reporting structure? These issues must be written in a formal document that defines the department, its purpose, and its goals.

Set goals and strategies. Engage in a process of goal setting that establishes the hopes for the department. Whom do you plan to reach (age groupings, persons inside or outside the church, disabled populations, women or men)? What outreach methods will you use to attract these groups?

Agree on a definition of success. This is an evaluation process. What is your definition of success (include this definition in organizational documents)? How will you know that you have reached your goals? See Chapter Thirteen for more information about assessing Christian education programs.

Assign work groups. Work groups allow the department to get its work done efficiently. They can be assigned to conduct assessments, design new classes, and determine the best training methods for volunteer teachers.

Define required tasks. Based on church mission and Christian education goals, define the tasks that are required to produce an excellent program.

Establish a time frame. Each task and strategy should have an associated timeline so that it will be easy to evaluate progress toward goal attainment.

Identify persons responsible for task completion. Success results from a system of accountability. Encourage those with specific responsibilities to work according to relevant goals and timelines.

Involve the Entire Church in Christian Education

If we are to obey God's admonition that we study his Word, we must involve every church member in a meaningful aspect of Christian education. One way that this can be done is by setting policy that requires certain forms of Christian education for certain membership categories. For example, each new church member can be required to take the new members class and those interested in church leadership to take leadership development classes. Most importantly, church members are going to be excited about participating in Christian education if they understand it to be vital to their salvation, important to the local church, capable of meeting their personal goals, interesting, informative, and enjoyable. (See Chapter Six, "Teachable Moment: Faith Mountain," and Chapter Fourteen, "Creating Vibrant and Meaningful African-Centered Christian Education: Chicago's Trinity United Church of Christ.")

Recruit, Train, and Retain Christian Education Teachers

Teaching is a gift that involves a wish to improve the lives of others by providing information and teaching skills that increase their options and opportunities. Teaching skills include the ability to communicate information effectively, the capacity to develop relationships that enhance individual and group learning, and the determination to prepare oneself to teach through a lifelong course of dedicated study. As possessors of the spiritual gift of teaching, Christian educators are those who feel a call to serve Christ by teaching his people. Christian educators engage their gifts as a strategy for personal maturation in Christ and make Christ available to others by providing them with sound theology and practical strategies for applying Christian principles to their lives. Successful departments of Christian education are those with strategies for recognizing and embracing those in their congregations who are called to teach.

Recruit Christian educators. On a regular basis, seek Christian educators through announcements, church newsletters, and bulletins. Identify persons in classes who appear to have this spiritual gift and encourage them to consider Christian teaching or administration. Hold events to attract new teachers and administrators. Use spiritual gifts assessments as part of classes, encouraging active participation for those whose scores reflect a teaching gift. (For on- and offline spiritual gifts tests and descriptions, see www.cforc.com/sgifts.html or www.google.com, keywords: spiritual gifts.)

Establish guidelines for teachers. Christian education departments should establish guidelines designed to standardize training requirements for Christian teachers, expectations for performance, and evaluation schedules.

Train Christian educators. It is the task of the Christian education department to make certain that teachers are adequately trained to teach. Most Christian education teachers are volunteers, many of whom have limited formal training in teaching. Christian educators must learn how to teach specific age groups and to use strategies that are interesting for persons with different learning styles. The organizational structure of the Christian education department must reflect a commitment to training. Training courses, taught by experienced Christian educators, should be required for all who wish to teach in the church. Section Three provides comprehensive strategies for Christian teaching to different age and ability groups.

Retain Christian educators. Celebrate excellence in Christian teaching and department administration on a regular basis. Despite the fact that Christian educators teach based on a calling, an identified spiritual gift, and with a purpose to work for Christ, they may not continue to teach if the department of Christian education is disorganized, does not actively value their contributions, or is peopled with staff who do not behave in accordance with Christian principles.

Market Your Christian Education Program

Christians are charged with spreading the good news about our Lord and Savior. Once Christian teachers have been identified and trained, it is time to announce new Christian education offerings to church members and people in the surrounding community. Use available technology (website, radio, and television ads), door-to-door appeals, in-church announcements, handouts that describe the exciting courses that your work groups have designed, and all creative outlets at your disposal to get people involved in Christian education.

Surveys indicate the importance of making a special effort to gain the interest of persons who have not traditionally attended Sunday school, Bible study, or other programs. Finding out what has kept them out of Christian education can provide important clues to the types of programs that must be designed to attract their interest.

Notes

1. *Lyle E. Schaller.* What Have We Learned? Lessons for the Church in the 21st Century. *Nashville: Abingdon Press, 2001, page 46.*

2. A Procedural Manual on How to Organize the Church for Christian Education. *Nashville: Townsend Press, 2000, page 5.*

3. *"The African American Experience" in* Holy Bible: The African American Jubilee Edition. *New York: American Bible Society, 1999, page 25.*

4. *"The African American Experience" in* Holy Bible, *page 27.*

HE'LL UNDERSTAND AND SAY "WELL DONE"

The Importance of Evaluation in Christian Education

We won't leave here like we came, in Jesus' name.
Bound, oppressed, afflicted, sick or lame,
For the Spirit of the Lord is still the same.[1]

THOUGH THE SPIRIT OF THE LORD REMAINS THE SAME, OUR PROGRAMS for teaching about Christ change over time in order to address the growing learning needs of our congregations and in response to social dilemmas that require that we provide for our members new sources of strategic support. To determine whether our Christian education programs, venues, and formats are meeting their goals, departments of Christian education have available to them a variety of techniques for evaluating whether their teaching objectives have been successfully met.

Why Assess?

Assessment pushes us to plan our programs well and then facilitates our efforts to determine the degree to which we have met our plan's objectives. Assessment is a tool that allows us to:

- Learn about the effectiveness of our Christian education programs
- See what groups within our congregation are being reached by our efforts
- Evaluate the ways in which Christian education programs match the church's mission
- Determine the satisfaction of the congregation with Christian education offerings

- Understand the reasons that parishioners participate or choose not to participate in Christian education activities
- Address the training needs of Christian educators

Assessment Strategies

Do it yourself. Though Christian educators have lives outside of the church and a number of demands on their time, it can be cost effective to use Christian education staff with skills in this area to conduct assessments of teaching programs, teaching staff, and church member satisfaction with Christian education activities.

Hire a consultant. Communities often have African American and other consultants who specialize in working with church groups, evaluating their programs at reasonable rates.

Seek volunteers. Students in social science departments at local colleges and universities are often willing to work on assessment projects at no cost as part of their training. Students are always supervised in their work by professionals with extensive experience in evaluating programs in nonprofit organizations.

Identify church experts. There are possibly members of your congregation who are trained at evaluation methods. As a tithe of their talents, they can design evaluation tools (surveys and questionnaires), conduct focus groups, tabulate findings, and make reports that provide Christian education administrators and teachers with the information that they need to achieve excellence in their programs.

Assessing Christian Education Needs within the Church

To understand whether current courses are meeting congregational needs as well as to determine what concerns can be met by new offerings, it is important to conduct a Christian education assessment. Determined by focus group interviews or distributed as surveys in worship, classes, and electronically, this assessment can address:

- Who attends Christian education courses and why
- What categories of courses they attend (e.g., Bible study, life strategies, stewardship, relationship issues)

- What classes they would like to see offered, at what times and on what days
- What factors encourage their participation in Christian education or discourage them from active participation

Assessing the Skills of Christian Educators

Teaching is a continuous process of learning. In the context of the African American church it is also frequently a process of retraining our understanding of our history as Africans in the diaspora, its seminal connections to our Christian history, and our place in it. Trained Christian educators will require refresher courses provided by their department of Christian education to routinely provide them with new information that can enhance and enrich their teaching. The department should also establish procedures for assessing their teaching staff on a regular basis.

Self-assessment. Christian educators should assess themselves following the completion of every course. This can be done as a personal assessment or as part of a more formal process. Important questions include, "Did I the meet the teaching objectives of the course?" "Did my teaching strategies reach the needs of those with different learning styles?" "Did I accurately represent the African presence in the Bible?" "Was course content aligned with the church's mission?" and "How might I teach this course better the next time?"

Departmental assessment. Though such evaluation is time consuming, some churches may wish to engage in a formal process of teacher assessment on a semi-annual or annual basis, asking a similar set of questions to those listed above.

Assessing the Success of Christian Education Programs

The ultimate success of the Christian education department is determined by its capacity to provide courses and programs on topics and in venues that meet the desires and learning needs of the congregation and that are aligned with the mission of the church. In the African American context this means designing excellent programs that honor our complex history, correct misinterpretations of past events, and honor values and traditions. Global assessments of program success occur in several ways:

Assessment of administrative processes. While individual classes can be successful because they are taught by gifted and committed educators, a truly successful department of Christian education effectively designs, coordinates, monitors, and assesses all aspects of their programs in accordance with an established work plan. To determine whether the work planning and administrative processes are working effectively, it is important to determine:

- Administrative positions. Are administrative leadership positions filled? Is there an organizational chart that has been approved?
- Planning processes. Is there a work plan? Are work plan time lines being met?
- Budget goals. Is there a budget, and has it been submitted to the appropriate authority for approval? Are there sufficient budgetary and staff resources?

Assessment of course offerings. Courses, seminars, and workshops can be assessed when the term is completed. A basic questionnaire can ask respondents:

- What personal learning needs were met by the class (include space for written response)
- Whether the class time was convenient (yes/no), and, if not, what times would work better (include space for written response)
- What teacher skills were most effective (provide list of options and several blanks for additional student categories)
- What teacher skills and strategies were least effective (provide list of options and several blanks for additional student categories)
- Would they recommend this class to others (yes/no)

Careful assessment of administrative processes, educator skills, and participant viewpoints help Christian educators make decisions concerning the best ways to carry out their mission to teach God's Word.

Note

1. *"We Won't Leave Here Like We Came." Rev. Maceo Woods in* African American Heritage Hymnal. *GIA Publications, 2001, page 407.*

UNASHAMEDLY BLACK AND UNAPOLOGETICALLY CHRISTIAN

African-Centered Worship at Chicago's Trinity United Church of Christ

Our roots in the Black religious experience and tradition are deep, lasting and permanent. We are an African people, and we remain "true to our native land," the mother continent, the cradle of all civilization. God has superintended our pilgrimage through the days of slavery, the days of segregation and the long nights of racism. It is God who gives us the strength and courage to continuously address injustice as a people, as a congregation and we constantly affirm our trust in God through the cultural expression of Black worship services and programs which address the Black community.[1]

IT IS SUNDAY MORNING, 11:00 A.M., THE SECOND OF THE THREE worship services that are held each week for the 8,000 families that comprise the membership of Trinity United Church of Christ. The summer heat swelters but congregants are comfortably dressed; the entire 250-voice choir, most ministers in the pulpit, and many members of the congregation wear brightly colored African garb. The sanctuary is a bright and open space, its carpeting and pew coverings are bright red. The altar, draped in kente cloth, holds a large open Bible. It sits beneath the sunlit midpoint of a transverse cross that serves as the sanctuary's ceiling.

Liturgical dancers, dressed in flowing white, move rhythmically through the sanctuary, catching an array of colored light that streams through the stained glass windows, windows that tell the story of African and African American Christian history. Drums speak their own special language in accompaniment. Headed toward the altar, the dancers stop and, in perfect synchrony, stretch their arms to heaven as the sound system soulfully plays a gospel rendition of "Joyful, Joyful."

Soul Fruit, a group of three young male recording artists from Houston, are next in the order of worship, pausing before they sing to acknowledge their thankfulness for being included as part of the service and their devotion to Christ. The senior pastor, the Rev. Dr. Jeremiah A. Wright Jr., who has earlier accompanied the Trinity choir on the conga drums and the keyboards, thanks Soul Fruit for the way that their music ministers to youth. Looking around the congregation, he asks for prayers for those who are sick, calling them each by name, noting as he does so the importance of being specific when we invoke God's name on behalf of those we love. He makes several announcements important to the activities of the church for the week. Then, looking out over a congregation that is clearly pleased to be in the Lord's house on this day, he smiles and says, "I LOVE you!" The congregation returns the sentiment. "We love YOU, Pastor!" This loving exchange is evidence of an almost intangible "something" that can be felt upon entering Trinity's doors. Trinity embodies its African values, practicing them in the context of its Christian activities and demonstrating, through love for Christ and each other, that the Church of God is a vibrant, vital, and welcoming family.

The Trinity story began in 1961. Part of the United Church of Christ, a historically white denomination that represents the merger of four traditions—Congregational, Reformed, Christian, and Evangelical—Trinity was envisioned by the Chicago Congregational Association of the United Church of Christ to be a racially integrated congregation. Because the community in which it was founded was entirely Black, the integration hopes, tied to the new political direction of the country, were not met. Instead, under the leadership of its first pastor, Rev. Dr. Kenneth B. Smith, Trinity "continued to be grounded in the experiences of African Americans even though its worship style was the style of the Congregational Church of New England."[2]

Trinity's history indicates that it has worked hard to become African-centered. A study conducted by Dr. Julia (Judy) Speller traced the stages of Trinity's identify from God consciousness to self-consciousness to its current identity as a mission-conscious congregation.[3] Formed at the beginning of the Civil Rights Era, Trinity experienced an identity crisis in 1968 during a time when, according to one of the city's leading journalists, the murder of Dr. King was "enough to make a Negro turn Black!"[4] The turmoil of the country was also experienced by the church, however, as they went through several "shifts in mission consciousness," a shift that led, over time, to a search for a new pastor, one who would be committed to African American Christian practice in radically different ways than had been their past experience. They found their new pastor, Rev. Dr. Jeremiah A. Wright, in 1972. Today, Trinity is driven by a clear set of African-centered values that undergird all of its work.

Committed to creating worship and Christian education experiences that are African-centered and relevant to the lives of congregants, the members of Trinity United Church of Christ proudly proclaim their identity as African American children of God. To those who wish to create African-centered programs of Christian education in their own churches, the pastor and Christian education staff of Trinity make these twenty-six recommendations:

Embrace Christ

1. Be Christ-centered. The most important value taught at Trinity is that Christ, the Son of God, loves us, and we, as he has instructed, must love others and ourselves as he loves us. All activities of the church reflect this belief and teach Christian theology.

2. Love Christ proudly. While some Christians may feel the need to hide their beliefs in public, Trinity's members are taught to state their love for Christ out loud as a step toward being unapologetically Christian.

Create a Holistic Definition of Christian Education

3. Define Christian education broadly. Trinity defines Christian education to include the entire educational program of the church. They provide a range of Christian education activities:

- *Sunday worship* occurs in a sanctuary that holds 2,500, with services at 8:00 a.m., 11:00 a.m., and 6:00 p.m
- *Youth church services* are held Sundays during all morning services
- *Saturday church school* provides an array of classes for young Christian learners
- *Adult Bible classes* offer twenty-two weekly learning opportunities
- *Music ministry* provides child, young adult, and adult choirs for those who wish to serve through choral praise
- *Spiritual retreats* held by the seventy church ministries provide opportunities for refreshing the meaning and purpose of individual ministries, establishing the ways each ministry meets its goals in line with the church's mission and Christ's teachings, training church members to better do ministry work, facilitating prayer and reflection, and establishing guidelines for personal ministry commitments
- *Leadership development training* occurs in meetings with deacons and other church leaders, and during a biennial churchwide leadership conference
- *Pizza with the pastor* is a teen meeting held two to three times each year in which the pastor discusses with them what it means to be an African American teenager in the twenty-first century
- *African American History Month lecture series* presents prominent ministers, teachers, philosophers, and social observers
- *Guest ministers,* all of whom are seminary trained and some of whom are seminary professors, preach throughout the year, bringing new views and perspectives to the congregation
- *Conferences* for women, men, singles, and married couples are held throughout the year to address group-related needs
- *Tutorial programs* in reading, math, and computer skills are offered to members
- *Confirmation class/discipleship class training* encompasses a year-long program for twelve- and thirteen-year-olds who are preparing for "admission" into adult Christian responsibility
- *Mission study trips* involve ministry groups such as the Africa Ministry and the Caribbean Connection, which provide trips to Africa, Brazil, and the Caribbean to study the culture and religion of Africans in the diaspora

- *Special ministries* such as the Domestic Violence Ministry, the Justice Ministries, and political forums educate members about Christian responsibility in the civic arena. Additionally, their listing in the church's roster of helping ministries alerts church members to the importance of learning about and addressing these issues through a lens reflecting Christian beliefs, values, and behaviors

Administer Effectively

4. Be visionary. The Ten Point Vision of the church reflects Trinity's values and their commitment to building God's kingdom by being a church that is worshipful, spirit-filled, prayer-filled, tithing, Bible-based, progressive, politically aware and active, love-centered, stronger-working, and community- and liberation-conscious.

5. Be consistent in presenting the church's message. Ministers, Christian educators, and all staff at Trinity are attracted to the church because of its mission and vision. Nonetheless, they too receive extensive training by the senior pastor and the Christian education team that re-examines their religious and historical learning, assures that they present a clear and consistent message to congregants, and are personally dedicated to the church's mission, vision, and unapologetically Afri-Christian approach. "We must," says Dr. Judy Speller, director of Christian education and professor of church history at a local seminary, "shape situations and symbols that reflect our African heritage. We must be vigilant, aware of our identity and how it affects our world views. We cannot just celebrate history. We must be African-centered and self-aware."[5]

6. Provide materials that teach. At Trinity, even the worship program is a learning tool. A colorful booklet with a cover depicting one of the stained glass panels in the church details the order of worship, including choir and congregational songs, Scripture, and the sermon speaker and topic. The pastor's page of the program provides important information for congregational consideration. The rest of the booklet lists unison prayers, provides the words to congregational songs, notes the week's calendar and upcoming activities at the church and in the community, has space for sermon notes, and reports on members who are sick and shut in.

7. Monitor the Christian education budget and related activities. Says Rev. Ann Patton, minister of Christian education, one essential job of Christian education departments is to design budgets that meet the learning needs of all of their ministries, coordinate intra- and inter-ministry learning activities to reduce redundancy, and assess the degree to which programs have met their mission-related goals.[6]

Be African-Centered

8. Embrace a Black value system. TUCC adopted the Black Value System, written by church member Vallmer Jordan in 1981. They believe in the following precepts and covenantal statements:[7]

- Commitment to God. "The God of our weary years" will give us the strength to give up prayerful passivism and become Black Christian activists, soldiers for Black freedom and the dignity of all humankind.
- Commitment to the Black community. The highest level of achievement for any person must be a contribution to the strength and continuity of the community.
- Commitment to the Black family. Membership in a strong family unit is essential for developing a sturdy character, capable of withstanding the forces of a racist society. The Black family circle must generate strength, stability, and love, despite the presence of negative external influences, and must extend that blessing to the less fortunate, especially to the children.
- Dedication to the pursuit of education. We must forswear anti-intellectualism. Continued survival demands that each Black person be developed to the utmost of his or her mental potential despite the inadequacies of the formal education process. "Real education" fosters understanding of ourselves as well as of every aspect of our environment. Also it develops within us the ability to fashion concepts and tools for better utilization of our resources and more effective solutions to our problems.

Since the majority of Blacks have been denied such learning, education must include elements that produce high school graduates with marketable skills, a trade or qualifications for apprenticeships, or proper preparation for college. Basic education for all

Blacks should include mathematics, science, logic, general semantics, participative politics, economics and finance, and the care and nurture of minds.

- Dedication to the pursuit of excellence. To the extent that we individually reach for, even strain for excellence, we increase, geometrically, the value and resourcefulness of the Black community. We must recognize the relativity of one's best; this year's best can be bettered next year! Such is the language of growth and development. We must seek to excel in every endeavor.

- Adherence to the Black work ethic. To accomplish anything worthwhile requires self-discipline. We must be a community of self-disciplined persons, instead of perpetually submitting to exploitation by others. Self-discipline, coupled with a respect for self, will enable each of us to be an instrument of Black progress and a model for Black youth.

- Disavowal of the pursuit of "middleclassness." Classic methodology on control of captives teaches that captors must keep the captives ignorant educationally but trained sufficiently well to serve the system. Also, the captors must be able to identify the "talented tenth" of those subjugated, especially those who show promise of providing the kind of leadership that might threaten the captors' control. Those so identified are separated from the rest of the people by: killing them off directly and/or fostering a social system that encourages them to kill off one another; placing them in concentration camps and/or structuring an economic environment that induces captive youth to fill the jails and prisons; seducing them into a socioeconomic class system which, while training them to earn more dollars, hypnotizes them into believing they are better than the rest and teaches them to think in terms of "we" and "they" instead of "US." So while it is permissible to chase "middleincomeness" with all our might, we must avoid the third separation method: the psychological entrapment of "middleclassness." If we avoid this snare, we will also diminish our "Voluntary" contributions to the first two methods above. More importantly, Black people no longer will be deprived of their birthright: the leadership, resourcefulness, and example of their own talented persons.

- Pledge to make the fruits of all developing and acquired skills available to the Black community
- Pledge to allocate regularly a portion of personal resources for strengthening and supporting Black institutions
- Pledge allegiance to all Black leadership who espouse and embrace the Black Value System
- Personal commitment to embracement of the Black Value System to measure the worth and validity of all activity in terms of positive contributions to the general welfare of the Black Community and the advancement of Black people towards freedom (and liberation).

TEACHABLE MOMENT

Trinity United Church of Christ Mission Statement

Trinity United Church of Christ has been called by God to be a congregation that is not ashamed of the gospel of Jesus Christ and that does not apologize for its African roots! As a congregation of baptized believers, we are called to be agents of liberation not only for the oppressed, but for all of God's family. We, as a church family, acknowledge that we will, building on this affirmation of "who we are" and "whose we are," call men, women, boys, and girls to the liberating love of Jesus Christ, inviting them to become a part of the church universal, responding to Jesus' command that we go into all the world and make disciples! We are called out to be "a chosen people" that pays no attention to socio-economic or educational backgrounds. We are made up of the highly educated and the uneducated. Our congregation is a combination of the haves and the have-nots, the economically disadvantaged, the under-class, the unemployed, and the employable.

The fortunate who are among us combine forces with the less fortunate to become agents of change for God who is not pleased with America's economic mal-distribution!

W. E. B. DuBois indicated that the problem in the 20th century was going to be the problem of the color line. He was absolutely correct. Our job as servants of God is to address that problem and eradicate it in the name of Him who came for the whole world by calling all men, women, boys, and girls to Christ.

9. Use language strategically. Trinity members learn to value each other as children of God and as African Americans. As a result, members are discouraged from using language that would hurt each other and undervalue their humanity. One such word is "middle-class." "We talk about income levels here," says Rev. Wright. "There is no such thing as middle-class for African Americans. You may make money and have degrees behind your name—those letters behind your name are how you make a living. The church is how you make a life. If you label yourself as middle-class, that means that you are acknowledging that others are lower-class. And who are those people likely to be? Your relatives? The language is divisive so we no longer use it."[8]

10. Live your mission. The mission of the TUCC, unapologetic about its commitment to its racial history, acknowledges the range of believers and worshippers whose differences are created by socioeconomic disparities, calls on the contributions of our heroes, and reflects their commitment to African-centered values.

11. Design a facility that honors history. Trinity's building reflects its African values in all aspects of its design and in the nature and function of the spaces it provides for worship and learning:

- Sanctuary design. Designed by African American architect Wendell Campbell and Associates, the sanctuary is a large, open, five-pointed star design, the building was first occupied in 1994. With the pulpit at the head of the star, the rows of pews are arranged so that every seat has an unobstructed view of the altar, the pulpit, and the choir stand. The sanctuary's balcony covers three points of the star and also provides clear views of worship activities.

- Stained glass windows. Designed by the Phillips Stained Glass Studio in Cleveland, Ohio, Trinity's windows tell the Afri-Christian story and Trinity's church history in four large panels. The first panel illustrates Egyptian monarchs who shaped the life of Moses, the life of Mary, Joseph, and Jesus in Egypt, and African and Old Testament stories, all serving as the background from which Christianity developed. The second panel depicts New Testament scenes including the crucifixion and resurrection of Jesus Christ. Our story as African Americans is traced in the third window, beginning with our Afri-Christian beginnings in North Africa and Nubia.

This window also depicts African Americans of different Christian denominations—Richard Allen (AME), Augustus Talton, the country's first African Catholic priest, and Henry McNeil Turner, an African-centered pastor who taught that Africans should learn their African faith origins. The fourth window illustrates modern African American religious heroes, including the ministers of Trinity. A videotape on the history reflected in the windows is available as a teaching tool.

- Village spaces. TUCC's building is designed with lots of open spaces, spaces that facilitate gathering. In effect, this creates a number of "villages" throughout the church, places where youth stop to chat, adults compare their work weeks, families gather for prayer, members cry and comfort one another when confronted with loss, and people laugh together, because that, too, is healing.
- Art. Trinity's walls are covered with art by Africans in America and throughout the diaspora.
- Trinity's Beliefs. Also on Trinity's walls are plaques that proclaim their mission, vision, and values as constant reminders for parishioners that praise of God and love of self are deliberate acts.

Plan Strategically

12. Plan for the long haul. Trinity is engaged in a process of long-range planning that is unique in its focus. The Board for Long Range Planning came into existence twenty years ago to develop a twenty- and fifty-year plan for the church. As they have reached their twenty-year goals, they are adjusting their planning processes, trying, based on research about future trends and the guidance of their mission, to imagine what their church will need for future growth in an increasingly global and technologically focused world. Part of this process involves succession planning, making deliberate decisions about the type of pastor they will need when Rev. Wright retires.

13. Use African-centered values to guide your strategic planning process. For any process to be effective at Trinity, it must reflect the mission and values of the church. Rupert Graham and Clementine Coleman, chair and vice-chair of the Board of Christian Education, respectively, note that their work involves understanding the mission and values of the church, orienting the bylaws to reflect the structure of the church and its programs, implementing the pastor's vision in line with the church mission, and strategic planning that establishes and supports the church infrastructure.[9]

14. Incubate the vision. With those values fully incorporated, the "job," says Dr. Iva Carruthers, a long-time planning board member, "is to incubate the plan, give birth to and carry the vision until it becomes an independent ministry. Our job is to ensure the longevity of the church."

Train the Next Generation of Christians

15. Teach your children well. It is important, says Rev. Michael Jacobs, minister to youth and children, "to share knowledge about our story, about our Afri-Christian roots in Northeast Africa so that our children can defend their faith in any setting," using accurate references (the Bible, Peters Projection maps) and the strength of their beliefs to guide them "now and throughout their lives."

16. Correct misperceptions. Teaching truth is more than providing correct information: it must correct misperceptions. "Africentricity," says Rev. Jacobs, "is not about wearing African clothes. Your head must 'wear' the culture."[10] The focus of much of his teaching, in conjunction with all teaching departments, is correcting the myths that "cause our children to look down their noses at others in the diaspora," rather than recognizing them as brothers and sisters who are children of God.

17. Support educational efforts. Children and youth are annually provided with a student planner that has a pastoral letter that challenges them to excel academically; gives important church information (hours of operation, church covenant, mission statement, value system, church history, pastoral vision for the year, and annual devotional theme and memory verses); provides academic aids (time management, rules of grammar, math resources, and geographically proportional U.S. and world maps); and presents a twelve-month date book that has monthly brain teasers to test knowledge of African and African American history, encouraging quotations, and a space for writing and monitoring personal goals.

18. Reinforce decorum. There are many new Christians entering our churches, many of whom may not be aware of what behaviors are appropriate in the church building or the worship setting. Trinity provides a brochure in which the pastor outlines church decorum in positive terms that describe why and in what ways the sanctuary and other church properties must be respected ("You are standing on holy ground!"), the roles of ushers in maintaining order, and the times when walking in the sanctuary is allowed.

Facilitate Congregational Study
19. Develop a Christian education curriculum based on African-centered values.
- The Center for African Biblical Studies. The Center offers between eighteen to thiry-two classes each quarter (ten-week sessions for Fall, Winter, and Spring; six- to eight-week sessions for Summer). It is recommended that students take courses in sequence to enhance the basic skills and African-centered informational base that will allow them to study Scripture in an organized manner.
- Church school. Programs for learners of all ages provide the basics of African-centered Christian belief and practice. Afri-Christian mapping is part of all courses at Trinity as is the use of storytelling to share African American Christian traditions.
- Drill Teams. Trinity utilizes Christian drill teams as a way to teach Scripture. From the tradition of fraternities and sororities, children, teens, and adults shout and stomp, citing Scripture when prompted by drill sergeants.

20. Provide appropriate materials. The Akiba, Trinity's bookstore, sells an array of Bibles, books on African American issues and African-centered Christianity, and all course-related materials. Books are arranged in sections that boast proud headings such as African Kings (books on African men in the diaspora) and African Queens (books on African women in the diaspora). Authors are invited to book signings. The store also provides cards and inspirational materials with African American themes.

Train Teachers to Teach
21. Value teacher training. According to Frances Harris, superintendent of the church school, teachers are trained according to the

Galindo model of Christian education (see Section One), learn African-centered mapping using Peters proportional projection maps, use tools such as the *African American Heritage Hymnal* and the *African American Jubilee Bible,* are trained regarding learning styles, and receive reinforced study of the church values, mission, and vision in a mandatory four-session training module. Teachers for the Center for African Biblical Studies, administered by Deacon Shirley Bim-Ellis, are required to take a sequence of nine core courses, among which are Bible basics, the African presence in the Bible, and the African origins of Christianity.

Engage, Expect, and Exemplify Excellence

22. Be organized for excellence. As part of the bylaws of the church, the Board of Christian Education specifies duties that indicate their responsibility for the "scope of ministry, coordinating, and monitoring the Christian education focus (from an African-centered perspective), of each of the volunteer ministries and other related Christian education endeavors of the congregation."[11]

Be Unashamedly Black and Unapologetically Christian

23. Welcome new members into the family. Since June 1972, Trinity has proclaimed these words on the first Sunday of each month as a part of a liturgy of welcome to new members and a reinforcement of their African-centered Christian beliefs: "We, then, as members of this church, gladly welcome you to be a part with us in the hopes, the joys, and the labors of the United Church of Christ. We promise to walk with you in Christian love and sympathy and to promote, as far as in us lies, your growth in the Christian life. There is no task more sacred than the liberation of Black people! God has called us to this task, and hearing [God's] call, we say, 'Lord, here am I, send me!' We, therefore, joyously declare that we are Unashamedly Black and Unapologetically Christian!"[12]

24. Shout your credo from the mountaintops. The motto "Unashamedly Black and Unapologetically Christian" is on all of Trinity's materials, posted on its walls, emblazoned on T-shirts, and, most importantly, branded in the hearts of all of their members.

25. Be the breath of God. Sweet Honey in the Rock, an a capella musical group, sings a song called "We Are" that describes us as the "breath of God," a concept that is tied to African religious beliefs. Rev. Wright has spent a lifetime learning and celebrating the Africanness of our religious practice. He is dedicated, he says, to "teaching everyone everything that I know." His last words of wisdom in this interview come from his recent travel experiences and his related learning. In Hawaii, he met with a holy person (a *kahu*) who taught him that *howle* is essential to life. Translated, *howle* means "no breath, no God." Rev. Wright was ecstatic, because on a recent trip to South Africa he had learned the Zulu term *gumntu gbantu*, the breath of God.

26. Know that you can only grow through community. Taught early by his parents the importance of understanding that African-centeredness is essential to the religious practice of African Americans, Rev. Wright lives what he preaches. He travels with parishioners to places in the African diaspora and there studies religious traditions and practices. In his congregation and South Side Chicago community he teaches *umntu, gumntu gbantu*—an individual can only be an individual by virtue of being in relationship with others. That relationship is fundamental to the South African concept of *ubuntu* (community).[13] This is the same principle that the South African theologian John Mbiti uses when he says, "I am because we are and because we are I am." There is no definition of self apart from the community. In the Zulu expression, the principle is even more profound. It asserts that there can be no individual, relationship, or community without the presence of *Ntu* (God).

A young woman stands in the center of the sanctuary, before the altar, microphone in hand. "This," she announces, "is Forgive and Forget, a show that helps people resolve their personal conflicts." Another young woman enters, takes the microphone and begins, tearfully, to discuss having stolen from her sister and run away to Chicago where, after joining with Trinity, she finally had the strength to ask for her sister's forgiveness. Her sister, present in the sanctuary, but unknown to the penitent, enters, walks to her sister and, with a tearful hug, lets her know that the bond of family cannot be broken.

It is Monday evening, the second night of the youth revival, and one thing is absolutely clear. Worship in this place embodies all of its African values. The service has begun with the reclamation of family, the shedding of tears within the shelter of a loving community, and re-entry into the larger fold, the community of faith, the breath of God, who strive to be the people God expects. Thanks be to God!

Notes

1. *Dedication Article. Trinity United Church of Christ. Original 1981, revised 1992.*
2. *History of Trinity United Church of Christ, in Trinity United Church of Christ Student Planner 2002.*
3. *Interview with Dr. Julia Michelle Speller, Chicago, August 15, 2002. Also noted in* Unashamedly Black and Unapologetically Christian: One Congregation's Quest for Meaning and Belonging. *Dr. Speller's dissertation submitted to the faculty of the Divinity School in candidacy for the Doctor of Philosophy degree. Chicago, Illinois, December 1996.*
4. *History of Trinity United Church of Christ.*
5. *Dr. Judy Speller. Director of Christian Education, Trinity United Church of Christ, August 15, 2002.*
6. *Rev. Ann Patton. Trinity United Church of Christ Minister of Christian Education. Telephone interview, August 15, 2002.*
7. *The mission and vision of the church also reflect these values. The Black Value System is reprinted with permission.*
8. *Rev. Dr. Jeremiah Wright, Jr., pastor, Trinity United Church of Christ. Interview, August 13, 2002.*
9. *Interview with Trinity UCC Board Members, August 15, 2002.*
10. *Interview with Minister for Youth and Children, August 15, 2002.*
11. *The Bylaws of Trinity United Church of Christ, Revised 1998, page 1.*
12. *Dr. Julia Michelle Speller.* Unashamedly Black and Unapologetically Christian: One Congregation's Quest for Meaning and Belonging, *a dissertation submitted to the faculty of the Divinity School in candidacy for the Doctor of Philosophy degree. Chicago, Illinois, December 1996.*
13. Umntu *(an individual)* gumntu *(can only be an individual)* gbantu *(by virtue of being in a community). Interview with Rev. Dr. Jeremiah A. Wright Jr., August 15, 2002.*

SAVING SOULS
BY TEACHING TRUTH

Christian Education as the Means to an Essential End

We have heard the joyful sound:
> *Jesus saves! Jesus saves!*
Spread the tidings all around:
> *Jesus saves! Jesus saves!*
Bring the news to every land,
> *Climb the steeps and cross the waves;*
Onward! 'tis our Lord's command;
> *Jesus saves! Jesus saves![1]*

CHRISTIAN EDUCATION IS A MINISTRY. OCCURRING THROUGH THE course offerings of departments of Christian education and in every venue of church activity, it is a way to teach about Christ and, through that teaching, to make Christ real to those who have given their lives to him. Christian educators have received a special calling. They are asked to study God's Word intently, learning its important lessons and imparting them in novel and interesting ways to a variety of learners. These learners, the body of Christ who are part of our local churches, have different needs, different goals, and different levels of maturity in their relationships with Christ. Though they teach others, Christian educators are themselves continuing to learn about the manner in which God moves in their lives and the ways that they must shape their lives to his will.

African American churches have strong traditions of Christian education. Viewing secular education as a form of emancipation from the constraints of slavery and as a method to equalize painful social inequities, the founding of many black churches was closely tied to educational principles. "No other area of black life received a higher priority from black churches than education."[2] Christian education in the African American context has concerned itself with the liberation of the soul and with stabilizing and strengthening its parishioners and the Christian community through enhancing their understanding of the African roots of Christianity, the spread of Christianity throughout the African diaspora, and a strong acknowledgment that Christ is the champion of the oppressed and those who strive for social and spiritual freedom.

Ultimately, Christian education is a form of saving grace. It teaches God's truth and encourages us to use that truth to live responsible, productive lives built on Christian beliefs and principles. Beginning with the Word of God as taught in the Bible and extending to the provision of information that helps Christians apply Scriptural teaching to their lives, Christian education is essential to the growth of the Church of God, the strengthening of God's people, and the capacity of God's people to make life choices from a basis of Christian facts, beliefs, values, and practices.

TEACHABLE MOMENT

Jesus and the Paralyzed Man (Mark 2:1-5)

A few days later, when Jesus again entered Capernaum, the people heard that he had come home. So many gathered that there was no room left, not even outside the door, and he preached the word to them. Some men came, bringing to him a paralytic, carried by four of them. Since they could not get him to Jesus because of the crowd, they made an opening in the roof above Jesus and, after digging through it, lowered the mat the paralyzed man was lying on. When Jesus saw their faith, he said to the paralytic, "Son, your sins are forgiven."

This story discusses the determination of a paralytic man to be seen by Jesus. While the man desired healing, his main concern was to be in the presence of this man about whom he had heard so much. In this town were many people who had come to see Jesus, who was a visitor in a local home. Some who were in the room were greatly concerned that Jesus had so boldly stated his capacity to forgive sins. This, they knew, was something that only God could do. Concerned that Jesus was a blasphemer, some townspeople confronted him, indicating that they did not believe that he was God.

Jesus responded in an interesting way. He knew that even those who were silent doubted him. He also knew that disbelievers would think that it was easier to make a statement about forgiving sins than to actually make a paralyzed man walk again. To those who did not believe that he was God, Jesus proved his divinity this day. "He said to the paralytic, 'I tell you, get up, take your mat and go home.' He got up, took his mat and walked out in full view of them all. This amazed everyone and they praised God, saying, 'We have never seen anything like this!'" (Mark 2:10-12).

Hidden in this story is another statement about the faith of those who, in this setting, believed in Jesus as their Savior. The paralyzed man was not alone. He was surrounded by four friends who had noticed that the crowd in the house that Jesus was visiting was so large that it would be difficult for them to honor their friend's request to see Jesus. Understanding the importance of their friend's need to be in the presence of God, they looked for creative ways to get their friend into the house. They succeeded; *they tore the roof off!*

This is the goal of African American Christian educators, to bring souls to Christ by finding unexpected methods to teach God's Word and by developing relationships with parishioners that enhance their capacity to serve effectively as disciples of Christ. As Christian educators we must:

- Bring to believers, through strategies designed to meet their varied spiritual and learning needs, the redeeming love of Jesus
- Enrich our faith through the study of our unique Afri-Christian history
- Equip new and established Christians with the tools they require to make life decisions that aid their **salvation** and **sanctification**
- Meet the people of God on their Damascus roads[3] (Acts 9)

- Dare to do something radical to bring souls to Christ. As described in Mark 2:1-12, we must be creative, outrageous, and determined. We must carry the lame, the limping, the lost, and the longing, all beloved, to Jesus. Letting nothing stand in our way, we must tear the roof off!

This is our task as Christians.
It is our awesome responsibility as African American Christian educators.
We must do our jobs well.
Our congregations depend on us to help them with the process of discipleship.
Christ, our Lord and Savior, expects and deserves our very best.
Christian educators teach God's truth.
Jesus saves and is the Truth.
So let it be!
Amen.

Notes

1. *"Jesus Saves." Text: Priscilla J. Owens, 1829–1907. Tune: William J. Kirkpatrick, 1838–1921.* African American Heritage Hymnal. *Chicago: GIA Publications, 2001, page 558.*
2. *"The African American Experience" in* Holy Bible: The African American Jubilee Edition. *New York: American Bible Society, 1999, page 31.*
3. *The places where they find God and are converted.*

Top Ten Tips for Creating Innovative Opportunities for Christian Education

1. Coordinate Christian education with the church's mission.

2. Set attainable goals and establish work plans for Christian education.

3. Create a learning congregation.

4. Teach African-centered values and content.

5. Recruit, train, and retain Christian educators.

6. Conduct assessments to determine the impact of Christian education programs, teachers, materials, outreach, and techniques.

7. Find creative ways to interest church members and those in the community surrounding the church in Christian education programs.

8. Identify the special gifts and potential contributions of Christian educators.

9. Recognize faithful, innovative, and determined service among Christian educators.

10. Tear the roof off in your efforts to bring souls to Christ!

Preparation for the Journey

1. What strategies do we use to advertise our Christian education programs to church members?

2. What is our timeline for designing and implementing a standardized program of assessment for the services provided by the department of Christian education?

3. How do we maximize our efforts for outreach to the community surrounding our church?

4. How might we work with other local churches to coordinate Christian education programs and, in so doing, increase the numbers of people who can learn about Christ?

5. What are some innovative ways to illuminate the spiritual gifts of Christian educators?

6. In what manner shall we recognize the contributions of dedicated Christian educators?

REFERENCES

FOR INNOVATIVE AFRICAN-CENTERED CHRISTIAN EDUCATION

Developing Departments of Christian Education

Merrill-Jean Bailey. *A Procedural Manual on How to Organize the Church for Christian Education.* Nashville: Townsend Press, 2000. This book challenges Christian educators to move outside of established molds and create innovative programs that meet current congregational learning needs. Order from the Sunday School Publishing Board, National Baptist Convention, USA, Inc. (330 Charlotte Avenue, Nashville, Tennessee, 37201).

Alvin Christopher Bernstine. *How to Develop a Department of Christian Education within the Local Baptist Church: A Congregational Enablement Model.* Nashville: Townsend Press, 1995. The model described in this book facilitates the development of Christian education programs that enable the congregation to grow in its knowledge of Christ and adherence to Christian principles. Order from the Sunday School Publishing Board, National Baptist Convention, USA, Inc. (330 Charlotte Avenue, Nashville, Tennessee, 37201).

J. Deotis Roberts. *Africentric Christianity: A Theological Appraisal for Ministry.* Valley Forge, Pennsylvania: Judson Press, 2000. Discussing the origins, history, principles, and purposes of Africentrism, this book provides a theological assessment of Africentrism's relationship to Christianity.

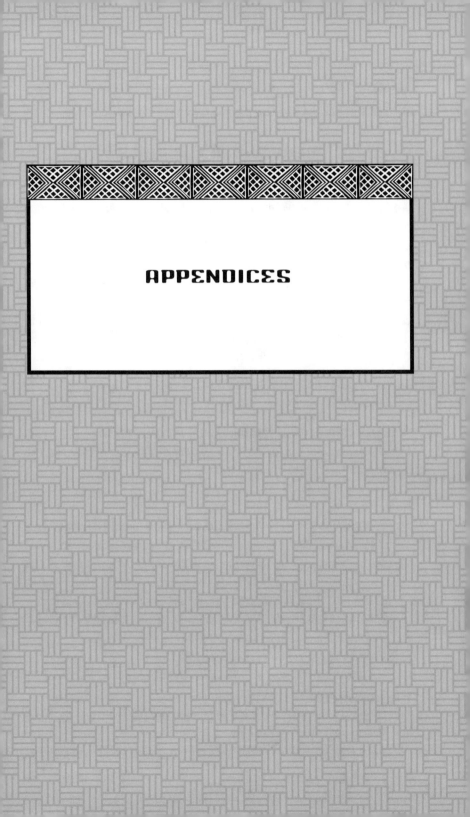

APPENDICES

APPENDIX 1

AFRICANS IN THE BIBLE

Christianity in Africa[1]

And the children of Israel heard say, Behold, the children of Reuben and the children of Gad and the half tribe of Manasseh have built an altar over against the land of Canaan, in the borders of Jordan, at the passage of the children of Israel (Joshua 22:11, KJV).

Mark, a northern African (Cyrenean) Jew and author of the Gospel of Mark, was from the city of Cyrene. A follower of Peter, he first proclaimed the gospel in Cyrene to other northern Africans who lived in the area now called Libya. He is considered to be the founder of the Coptic Church in Alexandria (Egypt).[2]

See Chapter One for additional information about Afri-Christian history.

African References in the Bible

Princes shall come out of Egypt; Ethiopia shall soon stretch out her hands unto God (Psalm 68:31, KJV).

Notes

1. *Information in this section comes jointly from a series of articles called "People of Color in the Bible," by Rev. Robert Ash, for www.blackandchristian.com (Search "Articles," accessed September 29, 2002) and Dr. Jeremiah A. Wright Jr.'s* Africans Who Shaped Our Faith, *Chicago, Illinois: Urban Ministries, Inc., 1995, pages 19–29. Both authors did extensive research that is noted in their bibliographies. When detailed information in this appendix comes primarily from one source, it is provided in a separate footnote.*

2. *Ash, "People of Color in the Bible: Part 2 (Ethiopia)."*

3. *www.encarta.com, keyword: Cyrenaica (accessed September 29, 2002).*

4. *Wright,* Africans Who Shaped Our Faith, *page 25.*

5. *www.encarta.com, keywords: Euphrates River (accessed September 29, 2002).*

6. *In many accounts of biblical history, Egypt is perceived as an enemy land that engaged in slavery ("Tell old Pharoah to let my people go!"). Egyptians who*

Table 9: African References in the Bible

Country	Text	Significance
Cush (Africa)	• Genesis 10 (see the Table of Nations) • Genesis 2:10 • Genesis 9:18-19	• Cush was originally broader than its current borders and included Africa. When the Bible was translated into Greek, Cush became synonymous with Ethiopia. • Cush is mentioned in the creation story; this country was home to black people of the Nile region, including southern Egypt and the Sudan. • Africans (Ethiopians in Greek translations of Scripture), were also called Cushites, the descendents of Cush, the son of Ham. (Ham was the youngest son of Noah.)
Cyrenaica	• Acts 2:10 (description of the region of Cyrene)	• Cyrenaica, whose capital city is Cyrene, is the biblical name of the country now known as Libya. Cyrenaica bordered Egypt (west) and was situated between the Mediterranean and northern Africa.[3] Though today Libya is considered to be an Arab nation, Arab peoples moved into Africa around the 7th century, 600–1,000 years after the compilation of the Bible.
Eden	• Genesis 2:10	• Research by biblical scholars indicates that one of the ancient names for Africa was Eden (as in the Garden of Eden).[4] The garden was also the starting point for the world's four largest rivers: the Pison which encompassed Havilah (Ethiopia), Gihon (Ethiopia), Hiddekel (Assyria, encompassed Mesopotamia, Babylonia, and parts of Eqypt; today these lands are called Egypt and Iraq), and the Euphrates (the river, once in Mesopotamia, now runs through Iraq, Syria, and Turkey).[5]
Egypt[6]	• Genesis 10:6	• The ancient name for Egypt is Mizraim, named for Mizraim,[7] the son of Ham (the father of the African peoples).
Ethiopia	• Genesis 2:11	• Havilah is the ancient name for Ethiopia.
Lands of Ham	• Genesis 6:10 • Genesis 9:18 • Genesis 1-20	• The word *Ham* is an English translation of the Hebrew word *KMT*, which is a translation of the African word kemit, the name that ancient Egyptians used to identify themselves.[8] This large region included Sudan, Havilah (Ethiopia), Mesopotamia, parts of Canaan, and all the lands of Egypt, including Nubia (southern Egypt).[9]

Africans in the Bible[10]

God *"hath made of one blood all nations of men for to dwell on all the face of the earth, and hath determined the times before appointed, and the bounds of their habitation"* *(Acts 17:26, KJV).*

Table 10: Africans in the Bible

Name	Text	Country of Origin	History
Asenath	Genesis 37 Genesis 39–47 Genesis 41:45	Egypt	Daughter of Potiphera, a priest in "the city of the sun," Heliopolis.[11] Asenath was Joseph's wife when he was ruler of Egypt; her love helped him through his difficulties as king (Genesis 41:51).
Moses' Cushite wife	Numbers 12:1-5	Ethiopia	After the death of his first wife, Zipporah (a woman of African descent; see page 194), Moses married an Ethiopian woman.
Ebed-Melech or Ebedmelech, also known as "the Ethiopian eunuch"	Jeremiah 38:4-15 Jeremiah 39:15-18 Jeremiah 13:23 (Jeremiah's description of Ethiopians)	Ethiopia	This Ethiopian eunuch saved the life of the prophet Jeremiah by rescuing him from the pit where he had been placed by his enemies. Eunuchs were surgically emasculated men who were expected to "stay in their place" as protectors of royal women. Ebed-Melech overcame societal views of his position and foiled the enemy's plan by doing the right thing.
Ephraim	Genesis 46:20 Genesis 48:1-20 Numbers 1:32-33	Egypt	Brother of Manesseh, Ephraim is the half-African (Egyptian) son of Asenath and Joseph who "fathered" one of the tribes of Israel (Numbers 7:48).
Ham[12]	Genesis 10:1,6	Cush	"Father" of the African peoples, whose name is listed in the Table of Nations (Genesis 10). Ham's relationship with Egypt is noted in Psalm 78:51. Genesis 10:1 describes how the ancestors of Shem and Ham are related.

Name	Text	Country of Origin	History
Jethro[13]	Exodus 2:1-22 Exodus 18:1-12	African Midianite and Cushite*	A Midianite black man who was father to seven daughters, Jethro was part of a community that was run by a council of elders and was based on African values. The Midianites, a successful group that had trade relationships throughout the ancient world, were not under the control of the city-states managed by the Hyksos. Jethro, who was also related to Moses (Exodus 2:11-21) was known in Hebrew as Raguel or Reuel, "the friend of God"; he played an important role in the founding of the lands that became ancient Israel (Exodus 18).[14]
Jesus	Revelation 1:10-19 Hebrews 12:1-2	Bethlehem of Judea	Revelation 1:14-15 gives a physical description of Jesus: his hair is wooly and his feet are (colored) like brass. Jesus was a descendent of Abraham on his mother's side. Abraham was from Ur of Chaldeas, an ancient African country (Matthew 1:1).
Manasseh	Genesis 46:20 Genesis 48:1-20	Egypt	The half-African (Egyptian) son of Asenath and Joseph who "fathered" one of the tribes of Israel (Numbers 26:29-34). His brother is Ephraim (see Ephraim above).
Mixed Multitude	Exodus 12:38 Numbers 11:4	Egypt	A large group of mixed race persons came out of Egypt, lived in Israel, and worshiped the God of Israel.
Paul	Acts 21–22	Cilicia in Taursis	Paul, a Jewish disciple of Jesus', was from the tribe of Benjamin. The ancestry of this tribe extends to the Garden of Eden (see "References to Africa in the Bible: Eden"). Because of his dark skin, Italian soldiers mistook Paul for an Egyptian (Acts 21:37-38).
Peter	Matthew 27:32 Acts 4	Bethsaida of Galilee[15]	A peasant fisherman, first known as Simon, Peter fervently believed in the message and teachings of Jesus Christ and became a foremost preacher of his Word (Matthew 16:18).

* Related to Ham and noted as Ethiopian in modern versions of the Bible.

Table 10: Africans in the Bible (continued)

Name	Text	Country of Origin	History
Puah	Exodus 1:1-22	Egypt	A midwife who, with Shiphrah (see below), helped the Hebrew women give birth. Because they were God-fearing, they disobeyed instructions by the king of Egypt to kill baby boys. They loved "the Lord more than they love[d] the law of the land"[16] (Exodus 1:20).
Rab-shakeh	Isaiah 37:7-9	Ethiopia	An Ethiopian king who surrounded Jerusalem in battle and blasphemed God. God sent him back to Ethiopia and he was killed.
Shiphrah	Exodus 1:1-22	Egypt	A midwife who worked with Puah (see Puah above) and defied the Egyptian Pharoah's order to kill the baby boys that they delivered.[17]
Simon	Genesis 9:19 Genesis 10:1-20	Cyrenaica*	Simon was a descendent of Phut, the third son of Ham (Noah's youngest son).
Zephaniah	Zephaniah 1:1	Ethiopia	Zephaniah's father was Ethiopian ("son of Cushi"–Cushi means a man of Ethiopia). Zephaniah was a direct descendent of King Hezekiah.
Zerah	2 Chronicles 14:9-12	Ethiopia	Zerah, the warrior, led a million-man army, the largest army that Israel had ever fought against. He lost his battle.
Zipporah	Exodus 2:15-22 Exodus 4: 24-26	African Midianite and Cushite**	One of seven daughters of Jethro, a Midianite priest (see Jethro on page 193), who became the first wife of Moses, himself a priest. Her family was trained as livestock breeders and in metallurgic arts.[18] Numbers 12:1 describes concern that Moses had married Zipporah. Zipporah circumcised her son, Gershom, and made a sign of blood on Moses (Genesis 17:10-14).

* Now known as Libya.

** Related to Ham and noted as Ethiopian in modern versions of the Bible.

defied these negative stereotypes can be found in Genesis 39:1-6 and 41:9-13,
1 Samuel 30:1-5 and 9-20, 1 Chronicles 2:1-5,9,18,25,28,31,34-35.

7. *Wright,* Africans Who Shaped Our Faith, *page 46.*

8. *Wright,* Africans Who Shaped Our Faith, *page 46.*

9. *Information on Nubia is found at www.encarta.com, keyword: Nubia
    (accessed on September 29, 2002). An award-winning musical version of the
    downfall of Nubia (which describes Egypt's enslavement of Nubians to
    expand their empire by gaining access to the mouth of the Nile) is on the
    soundtrack for Tim Rice and Elton John's* Aida *(Purchase is available from
    online music stores such as www.amazon.com and www.bn.com.)*

10. *This list is likely to be incomplete, as information is often lost as a result of trans-
    lations of the Bible into different languages or through divergent biblical inter-
    pretations. The author challenges knowledgeable students of the Bible to do their
    own research that can enhance their understanding of Afri-Christian history.*

11. *Egyptian priests were highly educated, and the Egyptian mystery religions, in
    which Asenath's father was a priest, developed the universities of North Africa.
    In later years these universities trained the Greeks in subjects for which they
    now receive credit (an example is the Pythagorean theorem). See Wright,*
    Africans Who Shaped Our Faith, *pages 38–39.*

12. *The name Ham translates as "hot" or "heat" and comes from the African
    word kam, meaning "land of the blacks." See Wright,* Africans Who Shaped
    Our Faith, *page 149.*

13. *Jethro was an ancestor of peoples from the land of Ham (Cush, a grandson of
    Ham, was Jethro's father who descended from Ur of Chaldeas (an ancient
    African country). Genesis 25:1-4 describes the Midianites' origins. Jethro's
    Cushite references are found in Exodus 2:11-17,21 and Numbers 12:1. See
    Wright,* Africans Who Shaped Our Faith, *pages 79–91.*

14. *See Wright,* Africans Who Shaped Our Faith, *pages 80–82.*

15. *Galilee was then part of Megiddo, a province of Assyria (1 Chronicles 7:29).
    See Wright,* Africans Who Shaped Our Faith, *page 61, and www.encarta.com,
    keyword: Megiddo (accessed September 29, 2002).*

16. *Wright,* Africans Who Shaped Our Faith, *page 61.*

17. *This disobedience was enormously significant. In ancient Egypt, pharaohs
    were considered gods.*

18. *Wright,* Africans Who Shaped Our Faith, *page 97.*

APPENDIX 2

PRAYER FOR ALL AFRICANS[1]

Creator God, Our Father, Our Mother, Our Friend

We come out of our churches, our mosques, our temples, our shrines
And invite you to enter with us all into the sacred space
    of our hearts.
Where there is always light and where you are always present...

We come from the Four Corners of the globe where fate
    has scattered us
We come from the dustbins of history
We come from the slaughterhouses of hatred
We come from the horror-houses of slavery
We come from the trauma of colonization
We come bearing the burdens of our ancestors
    to this time and place ... in search of Redemption.

We come for Reparations of an unjust economic system
We come to Educate ourselves about the possibilities
We come seeking Development of a sustainable way of life
We come to ignite the fire of Evolution to a higher spiritual order
We come as the standard bearers of a new Moral order
We come in search of Peace
We come armed with the Truth
We come to topple the Ignoble
We come so that we shall Overcome
We come to build a new Nation of humanity
    in a time and space beyond race.

Great Spirit who resides in each and every one of us
Grant us the vision, the wisdom, the courage, the temperance,
    the patience, the forbearance, to carry on the struggle for justice
But most of all grant us the grace to love each other
    and to love ourselves as we seek to triumph
    in the war for the heart and souls of humankind,
    for with love all things are possible.

Creator God, Our Mother, Our Father, Our Friend
We acknowledge that we are Soul.
We acknowledge that we are One Nation.
Though we are many tribes, many clans, many peoples
We acknowledge that we are each the wave
We are together One Ocean.
Come reside in the churches, temples, mosques, shrines
    That we now build in our hearts
As we go forth in search of Redemption.
Selah.

Note

1. *Dr. Claire Nelson. Presented at the United Nations World Conference Against Racism, Durban, South Africa, September 6, 2001. This prayer, written to connect the spiritual needs of those of African descent, includes non-Christians. Used with permission.*

CHRISTIAN EDUCATION CONFERENCES

Auxiliaries In Ministry
Sponsor: Church of God in Christ
Attendees: Pastors, Christian educators, church and denominational leaders who minister in the African American context
Meeting time: Summer
Contact: (888) 882-5196 or COGIC Convention Services, www.cogic.com (See events)

Faith in Action
Sponsor: United Methodist Churches
Attendees: UMC, AME, AME Zion, and CME pastors, Christian educators, church and denominational leaders who minister in the African American context
Meeting time: Times differ based on region and conference affiliations
Contact: www.umc.org (go to Faith in Action link)

National Baptist Congress of Christian Education
Sponsor: National Baptist Convention USA, Inc.
Attendees: Pastors, Christian educators, church and denominational leaders who minister in the African American context
Meeting time: Annually in June
Contact: www.nationalbaptist.org

National Black Church Education Conference (ABC/USA)
Sponsor: American Baptist Churches
Attendees: Pastors, Christian educators, church and denominational leaders who minister in the African American context
Meeting time: Summer
Contact: (800) ABC-3USA or yvonne.carter@abc-usa.org

National Christian Education Conference

Sponsor: American Baptist Churches
Attendees: Weeklong event for professional and lay church leaders
Meeting time: Summer
Contact: (800) 558-8898 or www.greenlake-aba.org

National Conference for Pastors, Christian Educators, and Laity

Sponsor: Urban Outreach Foundation
Attendees: Pastors, Christian educators, church and denominational
leaders who minister in the African American context
Meeting time: Annually in September
Contact: 4533 South Lake Park Avenue, Chicago, Illinois, 60653

United Churches of Christ Christian Education Conferences

Sponsor: United Churches of Christ
Attendees: Pastors, Christian educators, church and denominational
leaders
Meeting time: Variable times based on regional schedules
Contact: www.ucc.org (See directory, conferences)

SURVEY LETTER

June 11, 2002

Dear Pastor _____:

Because you are pastor of a church that is known for excellent preaching, teaching, and service to community, I am writing to ask for your assistance in collecting information for my new book, *Christian Education in the African American Church: A Guide for Teaching Truth*. Planned for publication by Judson Press in May 2003, this book is designed to help African American pastors and Christian educators of all denominations create vibrant and meaningful Christian education programs.

According to Israel Galindo *(The Craft of Christian Teaching,* 1998), all that we engage in, from worship to Christian education classes to Christian life, is Christian education. *Christian Education in the African American Church* focuses on:

- the best practices for Christian education in traditional and non-traditional venues
- creative uses of technology in Christian education
- methods appropriate for teaching those at different age levels and different levels of Christian experience
- a brief history of Christian education in the African American context

My goal in writing this book is simple: to strengthen our opportunities to provide excellent Christian education within the African American church. I am committed to assisting in the development of congregations that are well-educated in a manner that enhances their ability to live their lives and do God's work according to Christian principles. I strongly believe that our churches require clergy, Christian educators, and laity who are well-prepared to work together to build the kingdom of Christ. I am hopeful that *Christian Education in the African American Church* will serve as a useful tool for developing, supporting, and augmenting Christian education programs and strategies in African American churches.

To this end, the help I would appreciate from you is the following:
- A response to the questions:
  - What is your definition of Christian education?
  - What is the most creative form of Christian education that occurs in your congregation (consider worship services and classes)?
  - In what ways is it Africentric?

  Your responses can be provided to me through whatever form is easiest for you (a phone call, a letter, or via e-mail to any of the addresses listed at the top of this letter).
- An opportunity to speak with your Director of Christian Education/Sunday School Superintendent at their earliest convenience for a conversation of no more than 30 minutes.
- Any documents you or your Director/Superintendent care to share that describe your Christian education curriculum (in general and for different age groups or those at different levels of Christian experience). These can be mailed to me at the address listed above.
- If possible, an opportunity to visit and observe your programs during the summer months.

Enclosed with this letter please find:
- Information sheet on *Christian Education in the African American Church: A Guide for Teaching Truth*
- Cover blurb for *Christian Education in the African American Church*
- Information about the author (from *Total Praise! An Orientation to Black Baptist Belief and Worship,* Judson Press, January 2003)
- Endorsements for *Total Praise*

I look forward to hearing from you at your earliest convenience and look forward to the possibility of learning from your work for Christ.

Sincerely,
Lora-Ellen McKinney

CHURCH SURVEY RESPONDENTS

Denomination	Church	Region	Membership
AME	First AME Church	West	18,600
Baptist	Greater Christ Baptist Church	Midwest	704
	Metropolitan Baptist Church	East	6,000
	New Birth Missionary Baptist Church	South	20,000
	Shiloh Baptist Church	East	3,500
	University Park Baptist Church	South	7,000
Disciples of Christ	Mississippi Boulevard Christian Church	South	3,600
United Church of Christ	Trinity United Church of Christ	Midwest	8,000 Families
United Methodist	Jones Memorial United Methodist Church	Far West	700

APPENDIX 6

CHRISTIAN EDUCATION SURVEY PARTICIPANTS

Church: **First AME Church**
Members: 18,600
Address: 2270 S. Harvard Boulevard
Los Angeles, CA 90018
323-730-9180
Website: www.fame.org
Pastor: Rev. Cecil Murray
Director of Christian Education: Rev. Joyce Randall, *Director of Christian Education*

Church: **Greater Christ Baptist Church**
Members: 704
Address: 3544 Iroquois Street
Detroit, MI 48214
303-924-6900
Pastor: Rev. James Perkins

Church: **Jones Memorial United Methodist Church**
Members: 700
Address: 1975 Post Street
San Francisco, CA 94115
415-921-7653
Website: www.jonesumc.org
Pastor: Rev. Dr. James McCray Jr.

Church: **Metropolitan Baptist Church**
Members: 6,000
Address: 1225 R Street NW
Washington, DC 20009
Website: www.metropolitanbaptist.org

Pastor: Rev. Dr. H. Beecher Hicks
Director of Christian Education: Rev. Tonya Burton, *Minister of Christian Discipleship*

Church: **Mississippi Boulevard Christian Church**
Members: 3,600
Address: 70 North Bellevue
Memphis, TN 38104
901-729-MBCC
Website: www.mbccmemphis.org
Pastor: Rev. Frank Thomas
Director of Christian Education: Rev. Nadine Burton, *Director of Christian Education*

Church: **New Birth Missionary Baptist Church**
Members: 20,000
Address: 6400 Woodrow Road
Lithonia, GA 30038
770-696-9600
Website: www.newbirth.org
Pastor: Bishop Eddie Long
Director of Christian Education: Elder Vincent Harrison, *Senior Director of Education*

Church: **Shiloh Baptist Church**
Members: 3,500
Address: 9th and P Streets NW
Washington, DC 20001-3318
202-232-4200
Website: www.shilohbaptist.org
Pastor: Rev. Dr. Wallace Charles Smith
Director of Christian Education: Rev. George Mensah, *Director of Christian Education*

Church: **Trinity United Church of Christ**
Members: 8,000 Families
Address: 400 West 95th Street
Chicago, IL 60628
773-962-5650
Website: www.tucc.org
Pastor: Rev. Dr. Jeremiah A.Wright Jr.
Director of Christian Education: Dr. Julia Speller, *Director of Christian Education*
Other Staff/Interviewees: Deacon Shirley Bim-Ellis, *Administrator, Center for African Biblical Studies*
Dr. Iva Carruthers, *President, Urban Outreach Foundation*
Clementine Coleman, *Vice Chair, Board of Christian Education*
Rupert Graham, *Chair, Board of Christian Education*
Frances Harris, *Superintendent of the Church School*
Rev. Michael Jacobs, *Minister to Youth and Children*
Rev. Ann Patton, *Minister of Christian Education*

Church: **University Park Baptist Church**
Members: 7,000
Address: 6029 Beatties Ford Road
Charlotte, NC 28216
Website: http://www.upbc.org/home.htm
Pastor: Rev. Claude Alexander
Director of Christian Education: Dr. Cassandra Jones, *Minister of Assimilation (New Members)*
Rev. Barbara Peacock, *Minister of Discipleship*

Banking: Paulo Freire's term for the "European" educational practice of "depositing" information into students, considered less effective than "problem-posing," in which students use deductive processes to arrive at solutions to problems presented in the classroom.

Christian references: Paulo Freire says that educators must, like Christ, be sacrificial. In this view, because people of color have been deliberately undereducated in many parts of the world, Freire pushes educators to give their best to their students.

Community of learners: A Freirean concept in informal education that places students and teachers in flexible roles. As they learn from one another, they become a community of learners who are equal in power.

Conscientization: A concept developed by educator Paulo Freire to describe the process of developing a conscience about the world and its people. For example, in African-centered Christianity, conscientization is reflected in the responsibility of believers for learning about the spread of Christianity throughout the African diaspora, participating in missions that serve Africans in the diaspora, embracing African-centered thought, and actively incorporating African and African American values and beliefs into faith traditions. Additionally, this process is engaged when we learn about and learn from cultures other than our own.

Cultural backsliding: Adherence to the culture of victimization.

Denomination: A religious grouping within a faith, a section of the Christian church that has its own system of organization and specific beliefs and practices that differ from those of other groupings (www.encarta.com, accessed September 10, 2002).

Didactic: Instructional lecture-based teaching style.

Distinctives: Faith beliefs and practices that establish denominations as unique from one another.

Divinity: God; the quality of being God.

Epistemology: The branch of philosophy that studies the foundations of knowledge.

Evangelism/evangelistic: The spreading of Christianity through preaching, teaching, and missionary work.

Experience: The Freirean belief that the process of learning is enhanced when learners share their experiences with each other.

Homiletics: The art of preaching.

Informal education: A method of teaching developed by Brazilian educator Paulo Freire to encourage learning through the use of dialogue. This educational method was considered revolutionary when it was developed because it sought to correct the deliberate undereducation of many people of color, and it viewed students and teachers as equals in the learning process. Also called popular education.

Liturgical year: A structured form of worship recommended by the denomination. For example, the Book of Common Prayer used by Anglican traditions provides specific prayers, songs, Scripture, and sermon topics for each Sunday of the year.

Neural fatigue: The tiring of the nervous system related to lack of rest or overuse.

Ordinance: A sacred ceremony of the Christian Church, such as baptism or communion.

Parable: A Bible story told by Jesus Christ that teaches a moral or a Christian value.

Praxis: An action that learns from and is connected to other values. Praxis is defined as using conscious thought to understand reality and the manner in which it impacts your life (the mathematical formula for praxis would be: reflection + action = praxis). In the African American Christian context, understanding who we are (reality) and our history (reflection) is praxis.

Popular education: See informal education.

Salvation: The event of being saved from sin by the sacrifice of Jesus on the cross.

Sanctification: The personal process of being freed (saved) from sin.

Tactile: Related to the sense of touch.

Tenets: A set of fundamental religious beliefs regarded as true.

Theology: The study of religion, particularly the Christian faith.